An Introduction
to Sociology

An Introduction to Sociology in Ireland

Bernadette McDonald

Gill & Macmillan

Hume Avenue
Park West
Dublin 12
with associated companies throughout the world
www.gillmacmillan.ie

ISBN-13: 978 0 7171 4031 2

Print origination in Ireland by TypeIT, Dublin

This book is dedicated to my niece and nephew,
Mollie and Dylan

Contents

Preface

This text aims to introduce students to the world of sociology. By introducing students to key sociological concepts, I hope to make it possible for them to apply these concepts to themselves in the context of their family setting, community and wider society.

This text, which is suitable for students studying for FETAC, BTEC and HETAC qualifications in the caring fields, aims to increase the student's understanding of social, economic and political arrangements in an unequal society. The text is learner friendly and will provide the student with an up-to-date knowledge of the sociological context of social studies.

The book is organised into twelve key chapters providing information to familiarise the student with the distinct discipline of sociology, with the major theoretical perspectives and methods used to produce sociological knowledge, and with the key sociological concepts and topics.

When working with individuals, it is important that social carers/students develop an awareness of, and respect for, the variety of human experiences in our society today. By writing this book, I hope to provide an introduction to issues that have become and continue to be increasingly critical as we go through the early years of the twenty-first century, and to encourage students to do so with critical reflection and thought.

Acknowledgments

This has been an exercise supported by my family, friends and colleagues. I wish to briefly acknowledge a number of people. My parents, Peter and Mary, my sisters, Jacinta and Pauline, my brother Brian and my brother-in-law, Liam! My oldest friend, Osama Elsadig. A huge thanks to my own friendship network and the wider tribe in general: Ciara Gaffney, Mairéad Kelly, Mary Dowd, Lorraine Cahill, Fiona Maloney, Maura Dunne, Irene O'Dea, Kit McBride, Bridget McGibney, Margaret Reilly, Mary Lynch McKenna and to all the rest of the wonderful staff at Cavan Institute. To Mary Coyle (Principal) and Gerry McKenny (Deputy Principal) of Cavan Institute. To Síofra Gavin who typed this text. Finally, to Marion O'Brien and Aoileann O'Donnell (Gill & Macmillan), without whom I wouldn't be writing this list.

1

Introduction to Sociology

CHAPTER OBJECTIVES

After reading this chapter you should be able to:

- define sociology
- understand sociology as a perspective
- trace the origins of sociology
- define key sociological terms and concepts: culture, status, role, social group, social institution, social stratification and social control.

SOCIOLOGY DEFINED

This chapter begins with an examination of what is meant by the term 'sociology'. The authors of *Sociology – A Global Introduction* (2nd edition), John Macionis and Ken Plummer, have defined sociology as 'the systematic study of human society' (2002:4).

The definition given by Restivo (cited in Tovey and Share 2003:16) describes sociology as 'a field of inquiry simultaneously concerned with understanding, explaining, criticising and improving the human condition'. When attempting to answer the question 'What is sociology?', Osborne and Loon (1999) say that 'sociology is about explaining what seems obvious – like how our society works, to people who don't understand just how complicated it really is'.

Sociologists (people who study sociology) attempt to:

1. understand how society works, and
2. explain why people do the things they do, in the way that they do them. (Marsh 2002)

For Donohoe and Gaynor, sociology is 'the scientific study of society that aims to look at the causes and consequences of social change and the principles of social order and stability' (1999:149).

These definitions show that:

- sociology is the study of human beings

- sociology is the study of interactions and relations among human beings
- sociology is a form of enquiry
- sociology is a science that requires the gathering of evidence
- sociology is a distinct academic discipline.

Sociology occurs when people start to address and question what goes on between individuals – how they relate and interact with each other. According to Babbie, 'Sociology addresses simple, face-to-face interactions such as conversations, dating behaviour and students asking a professor to delay the term paper deadline' (1988:3). Not only does sociology study how humans relate to one another at an individual level, it also looks at how institutions and formal organisations function. It looks at how whole societies function and the relationships (or non-relationships) between and among societies.

Sociology requires us to study how people live together, how we co-operate or compete when times are good or when times get tough. Because human needs and wants sometimes result in situations that put humans in conflict with each other, there is a need to create rules. The creation of rules is an attempt to help humans live together, an attempt to help establish some order in a world that would otherwise be chaotic.

Babbie in his 1988 work *The Sociological Spirit* also states that 'sociology is also the study of how rules are organised and perpetuated' (1988:4). While it is important to examine the rules that govern how people live together, we need to examine how they arise and how they change over time. For Babbie, sociology is also the study of how we break rules and why at times this is not always a bad thing.

While the above section outlines briefly what sociology is, the next touches on the approach we must take if we are to develop a sociological perspective.

THE SOCIOLOGICAL PERSPECTIVE

The sociological perspective offers us a way to view, understand and affect the world we live in. It requires that we stand back and start to question all that we have taken for granted. For Macionis and Plummer, 'using the sociological perspective amounts to seeing the strange in the familiar' (2002:4). According to Peter Berger (1967), 'The fascination of sociology lies in the fact that its perspective makes us see in a new light the very world in which we have lived all our lives' (cited in Marsh 2000:8). Most simply put, 'The sociological imagination requires us above all to "think ourselves away" from the familiar routines of our daily lives in order to look at them anew' (Giddens 2001:2).

To really be a proponent of this perspective we must give up the idea that the way humans behave is simply a result of their deciding to behave that way and accepting instead the notion that society guides our thoughts and actions. While this may initially seem strange and difficult to do, it is a skill we need to master in order to view the world sociologically.

Thinking sociologically requires us to see society as much more than a collection of human beings. Failure to do so and to recognise the power of social institutions that outlive humans means we will be unable to deal with important problems and opportunities in our own lives and in the world. An understanding of the power that society has in influencing our thoughts and actions can empower us to deal with the problems of the world.

Grasping the sociological perspective requires us to grasp the idea that 'who we are' is a function of the society we live in. By doing so, we will see how it can help us deal with the constraints of society. This can set us on a quest for answers that may prove invaluable.

Developing a sociological perspective will enable us to:

1. develop a new way of thinking; one that questions our familiar way of understanding ourselves
2. critically assess commonly held truths and allow us to see opportunities or constraints that affect our lives
3. empower us to become active participants in our society
4. recognise human differences and suffering that may influence our decisions to confront problems of living in a diverse world. (Macionis and Plummer 2002:9)

While there are clear benefits (mentioned briefly above), there are certain pitfalls and problems associated with the perspective that we must try to avoid. Because we are part of a rapidly changing world, it sometimes becomes difficult to study society as it too changes. Becoming aware of this will enable us to question research findings and statistics that might have been reflective of a particular society at a particular time but that may be out of date or invalid today. Because we are part of the world we study, it is important that we try to maintain some distance from it and not develop a view that holds our society's practices or our cultural views superior or inferior to another's. We must also be aware that the information we produce as sociologists, and the findings we present, become part of a society's knowledge and that too can shape the working of that society. Overall what is being highlighted is the impact of sociology on society. To help one understand the perspective it is necessary to examine it at the time and in the context it first emerged. To do so, a historical account of the development of the subject is necessary.

THE ORIGINS OF SOCIOLOGY

Sociology, the science of social life, is a discipline of relatively recent origin. It was so named by the French writer, Auguste Comte, in 1838, making it a product of the early nineteenth century (Tovey and Share 2003). When Comte first used the term less than 200 years ago, he was interested in developing a new way of looking at the world. Unlike the great thinkers such as Aristotle (384–322 BC) and Plato (427–347 BC), who tended to focus their thinking on imagining the ideal society, Comte wanted to go a step further. For him, this involved analysing society as it really was and he believed that it was only by doing so that you could try to understand how society actually operated. Unlike his predecessors and their approach to society, Comte's new approach was to be characterised by a buzzword, that being 'critical thinking'. Assertions about society must make sense, correspond to facts. Comte believed that in order to truly understand how a society actually operates there was a need to develop a scientific approach. Comte therefore was a proponent of 'positivism' and saw it as the 'search for order and progress in the society word' (Marsh 2000:15). 'Positivism holds that science should be concerned only with observable entities that are known directly to experience' (Giddens 2001:8).

Comte believed that when we were equipped with knowledge about how society operated, then people would be able to build themselves a better life and a better future. But why did this discipline emerge in that historical period? What was happening around Comte that resulted in his seeing a need for a new science?

By the time of the birth of sociology in the early nineteenth century, huge changes were taking place across Europe and North America that were having profound effects on the people of that time. These changes were a result of the Industrial and democratic revolutions that occurred at the end of the eighteenth and beginning of the nineteenth centuries. Comte himself was one of those being affected by these social changes. He was born at the end of the democratic revolution in his own native France and grew up in the early years of the Industrial Revolution that first hit Britain before spreading to other areas of Europe. Society as people knew it at that time was undergoing massive transformations. The introduction of technology and the new economic processes associated with the Industrial Revolution were altering forever the organisation of societies. The democratic revolutions were raising issues about the proper relationship between the individual and society while debating human nature and authority.

Social change was happening at a rate that had not been seen before and as a result people like Comte saw a need to identify these changes associated with modernity and to chart its likely path. By understanding what was happening one could build oneself a better future. Hence the emergence of the discipline of sociology (from the Greek and Latin words meaning the study of society) which Comte divided into two parts:

1. social statics, which looks at how society is held together, and
2. social dynamics, which looks at how society changes. (Macionis and Plummer 2002:12)

KEY SOCIOLOGICAL TERMS AND CONCEPTS
Culture

'Culture refers to the ways of life of the members of a society or of groups within a society. It includes how they dress, their marriage customs and family life, their patterns of work, religious ceremonies and leisure pursuits' (Giddens 2001:22). When people behave in a particular way, it is believed that their behaviour is determined by the culture they live in. Just as different individuals have different personalities, different societies have different cultures. For example, Irish culture is very different to Chinese culture.

Culture in its broadest sense is all the ways of behaving, interacting, thinking and communicating that are handed down from one generation to the next through language and all other modes of communicating, which according to Osborne and Loon include 'gesture, painting, writing, architecture, music, fashion, food and so on' (1999:142).

Although human culture is very recent, it is said to be the force that separates us from primitive ways of living. A society's culture is their way of behaving that allows them to make sense of the world. At the same time it makes sure everyone else knows what they are supposed to be doing. Cultures vary the world over, but despite huge differences they are found to be built on five major components:

1. symbols
2. language
3. values/beliefs
4. norms
5. material culture.

Status

Status refers to the social positions a person can occupy within a society or within a smaller social grouping (Babbie 1988). For example, in society a person can occupy the status of father, student, doctor, etc. Each of us in real life occupies numerous statuses and we act accordingly, because each status we occupy has certain kinds of behaviour associated with it. When you occupy the status of doctor there are certain kinds of behaviour expected of you that would not be expected of a disc jockey. Each status we occupy acts like a mask that we hold up when we interact with others, which determines our behaviour and the expected behaviour of another.

Throughout our lives we continue to learn the statuses we occupy, the behaviour expectations associated with those statuses and our relationship with people occupying other statuses. It is a process that continues right through our life cycle because during this time the statuses we occupy in society change. Our status as student ends when we finish study and enter the arena of work.

Roles

When we occupy a certain status in society, we have functions to serve. These are most commonly called the 'roles' associated with and expected of a status. Teacher, dentist, waitress are all examples of occupational roles, while grandmother, sister, son provide examples of family roles (Donohoe and Gaynor 1999).

Social group

Social gatherings of people such as an audience or a crowd do not constitute a sociologist's definition of a group. To be part of a group, members must agree on a number of characteristics springing from shared common interest or interaction with one another, have a sense of identity and have some degree of structure. Two types of groups have been distinguished by sociologists – primary groups and secondary groups (Marsh 2000:30).

Primary groups are made up of people connected to one another through primary relationships; relationships we have with people closest to us such as our family members or partner. On the other hand, the relationships we have within secondary groups are based on the statuses we occupy and the roles we expect of such statuses – such as that between a teacher and his or her student.

Sociologists are interested in how groups

1. contribute to our sense of identity, and
2. influence who people think we are.

Social institution

Sociologists speak of institutions when referring to the family, education, politics, religion and so forth. The concept can generally be applied to 'social aspects of social behaviour regulated by well established, easily recognised and relatively stable norms, values and law' (Mann 1983:172).

These norms, values and laws lead to the establishment of agreements that govern broad aspects of social life. The main function of institutions is to support the survival of the group by firstly shaping individual experiences.

Institutional change does occur and is most likely to occur when the beliefs and values of one institution come into conflict with another. Change can also be a result of conflict within the same institution.

Social stratification

Social stratification refers to 'a system by which a society ranks categories of people in a hierarchy' (Macionis and Plummer 2002:178). Most societies the world over have some form of stratification that results in some groups of people being in superior positions. Such positioning in a 'hierarchy' allows certain groups to enjoy considerably more power, prestige or access to resources such as health, education, etc. than others.

While every society (except the most technologically primitive) stratifies in some way, four main systems of stratification have been identified by sociologists. These are slavery, estates, caste and class. Each of these systems are made up of their own strata or layers. Your life chances or opportunities are very much determined by the position you occupy on these social strata.

Some of these stratification systems are open and some are closed. When we speak of an open system of stratification we are referring to a system that allows people to change their position on the hierarchical structure throughout their life course. The class system that operates in Ireland is considered an open system. A closed system does not afford a person the same opportunity and as a result a person's position in life is solely determined by the family group they are born into. The caste system that operates in parts of India provides a good example of a closed system of stratification.

Social control

When people do not abide by the rules or behaviour expectations of a certain society they are disciplined. Social control aims to create social order. It can take many different forms but falls into two broad categories – informal and formal.

Informal social control can be expressed in disapproving looks by another if something is said or done out of context. In contrast, more serious acts such as murder, theft or child abuse are disciplined by formal social control which is backed by the law, the Gardaí, the courts and the prison system. Other means of social control could possibly include psychiatrists and social workers.

The following chapters will deal with each of these concepts in greater detail, especially in relation to Irish society.

2

Concepts and Processes of Socialisation and the Acquisition of Culture

CHAPTER OBJECTIVES

After reading this chapter you should be able to:
- define socialisation
- distinguish between primary and secondary agents of socialisation
- briefly outline socialisation and the life course
- explain what is meant by 're-socialisation'
- define culture
- understand the components of culture – symbols, language, values, norms and material culture
- identify causes of cultural change.

SOCIALISATION DEFINED

'Socialisation refers to the way in which we absorb the rules of behaviour which are common in our society' (Abbott 1998:10). The process of socialisation involves learning to live according to the values and expectations of the society in which we live through experience and through relationships. The process starts when we are babies and continues right throughout our lives. Contact with other people affects how our personalities are shaped and developed. 'We come to behave, to feel, to evaluate and think similarly to those around us. Most societies tend to reproduce their social kind from generation to generation. However the process is complex and not fully understood' (Clarke *et al.* 2000:150).

The nature/nurture debate

One of the big debates that has been going on for centuries is the nature/nurture debate. In this debate, we are asked if the behaviour of people is due to their nature (or genetics) or to their nurture (or environment). Charles Darwin was one of the first who argued, during the nineteenth century, 'that each species evolves over thousands of generations as genetic variations enhance survival and reproduction. Biologically rooted traits that enhance survival emerge as a species' "nature"' (Macionis and Plummer 2002:152). This view enables us to exploit people. 'It is easy to exploit others if you think that they are not human in the same sense that you are' (www.usi.edu). However, these views were challenged by a psychologist, John B. Watson, in the twentieth century. He came up with the theory of behaviourism. His theory stated that human behaviour was not instinctive, but learned. Watson insisted that people differed only in their cultural surroundings, and from this theory we received the 'nature' idea.

'In today's world, we do not say that our behaviours are instinctual, but rather they are learned. What we do with inherited potential depends on our social experiences' (Plomin *et al.* 1980, cited in www.usi.edu).

According to Macionis and Plummer, 'We should not think of nature as opposing nurture, though, since we express our human nature as we build culture. For humans, then, nature and nurture are inseparable' (2002:152).

PRIMARY AND SECONDARY AGENTS OF SOCIALISATION

Primary socialisation: First stage of socialisation. It occurs in infancy and childhood and is the 'most intense period of cultural learning' (Giddens 2001:26). During this time children learn language, what constitutes acceptable behaviour and social skills which form the foundation for later learning. These are learned from those people who are closest to the child, i.e. parents, near family and main carers. These are referred to as the primary agents of socialisation.

Secondary socialisation: This stage of socialisation takes place in later childhood and maturity. At this stage children adapt to the wider world and learn to relate to a variety of people in a variety of different ways. Peers, schools, clubs, churches, the media and eventually the workplace become socialising forces for individuals. 'Social interactions in these contexts help people learn the values, norms and beliefs which make up the patterns of their culture' (Giddens 2001:28).

The following settings have special significance in the socialisation process:

The family

Often seen as the agent that has the most impact on the socialisation process. For the first few years of life children are totally dependent on their parents. During this time they are learning (consciously and unconsciously) from their parents. According to Macionis and Plummer (2002) 'The family also confers on children a social position, that is, parents not only bring children into the physical world, they also place them in society in terms of race, ethnicity, religion and class.'

Schooling

When children go to school they meet other children from different backgrounds than their own. They tend to form play groups with children made up of one sex and race. According to Best (1983), 'boys engage in more physical activities and spend more time outdoors, while girls tend to be more sedentary, often helping the teacher with many housekeeping chores, (cited in www.usi.edu).

Peer groups

Peer groups allow children to escape the direct supervision of adults. Peer groups are important as they help children form new relationships and develop their own identities. Topics such as girls/boys, music, etc., can be discussed more freely. 'Peer groups aid in the socialisation process because children in certain groups conform to the ideals of that group while disliking other groups' (www.usi.edu).

Mass media

The mass media has an enormous influence on the process of socialisation. For example, children can become socialised through the programmes they are allowed to watch on the television. While the media includes newspapers, radio, internet, etc., some research states that 'television consumes as much of children's time as interacting with parents' (Macionis and Plummer 1997:141).

SOCIALISATION AND THE LIFE COURSE

Socialisation is a life-long process. According to Macionis and Plummer, 'our society organises human experience according to age, resulting in distinctive stages of life, i.e. (1) Childhood, (2) Adolescence, (3) Adulthood, (4) Old Age' (1997:141).

Childhood: At this stage children are said to be free from the responsibilities of adults.

Adolescence: Refers to the stage of life between childhood and adulthood. Can be a difficult time for teenagers as they struggle to develop identities separate from their parents.

Adulthood: Often seen as the period of life when most accomplishments occur. During this time most people begin careers, start families, etc. 'During middle adulthood, between ages 40 and 60, people begin to sense that improvements in life circumstances are unlikely' (www.usi.edu).

Old age: This stage is defined as the final stage of life. Because of retirement or because they may be too sick to care for themselves, people at this stage may begin to depend on others. 'The growth into old age in our society means leaving behind past roles and becoming dependent again' (*Ibid.*:9).

RE-SOCIALISATION

This type of socialisation involves confinement in jails or in psychiatric hospitals. The reason for re-socialisation is 'because the people have done something wrong, and need to be socialised in order to go back and be a productive member of society' (www.usi.edu). The staff who work in institutions whose goal is to re-socialise are involved in a two-part process:

1. eroding the inmate's identity and self autonomy, and
2. building a 'new self' for the inmate through a system of rewards and punishments.

CULTURE DEFINED

Culture refers 'to the non-biological aspects of human societies – to the values, customs and modes of behaviour that are learned and not internalised by people rather than being genetically transmitted from one generation to the next' (Marsh 2000:24).

Different societies have different cultures. We learn the culture of our society through the process of socialisation. Despite differences in the cultures found throughout the world, they all seem to be built on five major components: symbols, language, values, norms and material objects.

THE COMPONENTS OF CULTURE

1. Symbols

'Anything that carries a particular meaning recognised by people who share a culture' (Macionis and Plummer 2002:100). Societies may develop their own symbols such as types of clothing, flags, logos, which will give particular codes to other members of the culture. These symbols convey meaning to the people of a culture. For example, in Ireland:

- the tricolour is a symbol of our national identity
- the shamrock is a symbol of our Christian heritage
- it is customary to wear black at funerals.

The pint of Guinness, the bodhrán, the GAA etc., are all examples of symbols in Irish society. 'We "read" these symbols as signs which guide our behaviour in particular situations' (Abbott 1998:8).

2. Language

The most obvious way in which members of a society share meanings is through using the same language. The modernisation perspective believes that 'modernising societies will become linguistically homogenous: within them everyone will eventually speak the same language, or at the very least, linguistic differences will decline as a significant source of division and conflict' (Tovey and Share 2003:332).

They go on to say that although this might be seen to have been the fate of the Irish language, as now the majority of the population of Ireland speaks English, the Irish language is not dead. Evidence for this includes findings from Ó Riagáin which state that:

1. 'The number of families that use Irish as the main language in their family circle is roughly the same today outside as inside the Gaeltacht areas with a particularly high proportion living in the greater Dublin region.
2. Most English speakers in Ireland today know some Irish.
3. The Irish language is still regarded as a central element in Irish national identity by a large majority of the population' (Ó Riagáin 1988, cited in Tovey and Share 2003:333).

'Groups of people with similar interests and outlook often develop their own language. Examples would be people in the same job, followers of particular types of music, people from the same social class or people from a particular area in a country or city. The slang and jargon which such groups use can serve to identify the members to each other and help to reinforce their sense of identity. When we say that people will "know what we mean" we are saying that meanings are shared' (Abbott 1998:8).

3. Values

'Values are the standards people have about what is good and bad' (Macionis and Plummer 2002:104). The values that a society holds in high esteem are reflected in the norms governing our everyday attitudes and behaviour. Values vary from culture to culture. 'Values are ideas that derive from beliefs and are about what is thought to be just, correct and proper. It is considered wrong to take another person's life but, in times of war and conflict, a person may be rewarded for killing people' (Donohoe and Gaynor 2003:239). In Irish society, areas given high value include:

- Christian values
- family values
- education
- work/status
- justice and fair play
- public safety.

According to Tovey and Share, 'the values of this national culture then increasingly converge with those of the advanced societies giving rise to a shared "world culture", in which nationalism and national cultural barriers are no longer significant' (2003:331).

4. Norms

'Norms refer to common and agreed ways of behaviour in various social activities' (Abbott 1998:9).

Some norms are formally established as laws. In Ireland we have laws prohibiting murder, robbery, rape, drink driving, speed limits, abortion, underage drinking. A US sociologist, Sumner, recognised that some norms are more crucial to our lives than others. He referred to these as *mores* – 'a society's standards of proper moral conduct' (Macionis and Plummer 2002:107). He believed that:

- mores applied to everyone, everywhere, all the time
- people developed an emotional attachment to these mores
- people will defend them publicly. (*Ibid.*:107)

Our behaviour is also governed by the non-legal norms of our society. 'These norms are basically "social manners". It is the norm in Ireland to shake hands when introduced to someone' (Donohoe and Gaynor 2003:239). These norms can also include notes about proper dress, common courtesy, etc. Sumner used the term 'folkways' to designate a society's customs for routine, casual interaction . . . In short, while mores distinguish between right and wrong, folkways draw a line between right and ~~wrong~~' (Macionis and Plummer 2002:107).

rude

5. Material culture

An important component of any culture is the material culture or the tangible aspects. To help understand the culture of a society we must view the objects that culture produces, 'the material goods, products, and the tools that people use in their everyday lives, e.g. cars, computers, books, clothes, tools. These objects are sometimes called "material culture" and can be used to indicate status or to make cultural or social statements' (Abbott 1998:10). All these objects that we use in everyday life take on a symbolic meaning.

CAUSES OF CULTURAL CHANGE

Cultural changes are set in motion in three ways: invention, discovery and diffusion.

1. Invention results in the creation of new cultural elements. Invention has given us the telephone, the television, the internet, etc. All these inventions have had a major impact on our way of life. This process goes on constantly.
2. According to Macionis and Plummer, the second cause of cultural change is discovery and 'it involves recognising and understanding something not fully understood before – from a distant star, to foods of another culture, etc.' (2002:110).
3. Diffusion refers to the spread of cultural traits from one society to another. 'The technological ability to send information around the globe in seconds – by means of radio, television, fax and computer – means that the level of cultural diffusion has never been greater than it is today' (*Ibid.*:110).

Through culture we attempt to make sense of ourselves and the surrounding world. 'Culture can constrain human needs and ambitions, yet, as cultural creatures, we have the capacity to shape and reshape the world to meet our needs and pursue our dreams' (Macionis and Plummer 2002:120).

3

Major Sociological Perspectives and Theories

CHAPTER OBJECTIVES

After reading this chapter you should be able to:
- explain what is meant by concepts
- talk about the founding of sociology
- describe the following sociological perspectives
  - structural functionalism
  - conflict theory
  - social action theory
  - feminism
- explain briefly the main theories of
  - Durkheim
  - Marx
  - Weber.

As scientists, sociologists are consciously committed to understanding how society operates. Sociology is an attempt to understand the purpose and experiences of its members from a sociological perspective. In order for us to do this, a key component in our way of approaching sociology and to appreciate it as an area of study is the ability to think critically. To think critically requires that we give way to logical reasoning. How do we do that? In part, this involves the development of theories. 'Theory → logical model specifying relationships among variables as an explanation for the way things are' (Babbie 1988). To understand the true purpose of theory we need to consider a few of its basics, that is, concepts and the relationships among variables.

CONCEPTS

'Concepts are mental images we use to bring order to the mass of specific experiences we have' (Babbie 1988:17).

By forming concepts we allow ourselves to group together similar things and at the same time to distinguish dissimilar ones. 'For example the concept "human being" groups nearly 5 billion creatures into a single category and distinguishes them from billions and billions of other creatures. Male and female divide the 5 billion human beings into two categories' (*Ibid.*:17).

Children, Asians, students, teachers are other examples of concepts that enable us to distinguish between different groups of humans. Concepts can also refer to ideas that do not always distinguish between groups of people. For example, when we speak of unemployment, depression, marriage, we are using concepts.

Along with carefully defining the concepts, sociologists seek to discover and establish order among concepts. The concepts Christian and Muslim are often referred to as attributes of individuals. The variable 'religion' is a concept bringing those two attributes together. Other examples of variables are gender, which is a concept that brings together attributes such as male and female, and nationality, which brings together attributes such as Irish and French.

While sociology is committed to discovering relationships among the variables that distinguish different kinds of people, for example, by asking the question 'Are married men happier than single men?', it does not stop there. Upon identification of such relationships, sociological theory attempts to develop a more detailed picture of the interrelations among a great many variables. By doing so, it is able to provide a greater understanding of social life in general. Many of the questions and problems regarding sociologists' understanding of social life remain similar to those raised by the founders of sociology. The approaches they use to help them do so remain the three major models commonly used in modern sociology and they act very much as windows to our world.

THE FOUNDING OF SOCIOLOGY: MARX, DURKHEIM AND WEBER

Karl Marx (1818–83), Emile Durkheim (1858–1917) and Max Weber (1864–1920) were among the first to look at society in what we have come to think of as a specifically sociological way. Like Comte who named the discipline, all three were interested in and wanted to understand the major changes that were occurring in Europe during their own time. Their attempts to do so were to have a major impact on the discipline of sociology. All three lived during the nineteenth century, which was a period of huge change. Revolutions such as the Industrial and political revolutions were bringing huge changes to the society they knew. They were changing how their society operated and as a result were having a huge impact on the experiences of its members. Marx, Durkheim and Weber wanted to understand and explain why such events and changes were taking place. To simply describe what was happening was not enough. They went deeper and by so doing they founded a new discipline – sociology. Durkheim, Marx and Weber had the common goal of examining society and trying to understand how it functioned and changed, but each one differed in his approach to doing so. Differences in their approaches led to their developing (separately) three different perspectives, all of which required a scientific approach.

SOCIOLOGICAL THEORY AND STRUCTURAL PERSPECTIVES

'At this stage all that we mean by sociological theory is the body of ideas, tested and untested, making up sociological thought' (O'Donnell 1992:7). According to O'Donnell (1992), in order to construct an adequate sociological perspective we need to be able to examine and answer some basic questions of sociological theory. It was upon answering such questions that Marx, Durkheim and Weber helped to produce three distinct traditions of sociological thought or perspectives, namely:

* structural functionalism, which owes much to Durkheim
* Marxism, which is associated with Karl Marx
* social action theory, which owes much to Weber.

For O'Donnell (1992:7), the seven key questions that need to be answered are:

1. How is society constructed?
2. How does society operate or function?
3. Why are some groups in society more powerful than others?
4. What causes social change?
5. Is society normally in orderly balance or in conflict?
6. What is the relationship of the individual to society?
7. What is the primary purpose of sociological study?

The three perspectives of Durkheim, Marx and Weber are structural in nature as they focus on how society affects individuals and groups rather than on how individuals or groups create society.

Structural functionalism: Durkheim

'Functionalism is a framework for building theory that envisages society as a complex system whose parts work together to promote solidarity and stability' (Macionis and Plummer 2002:22).

In other words, functionalists like Durkheim believed that for a society to survive, its various social processes must net smoothly together to meet the system's needs. According to Mann, 'Functionalism's basic question is "How does society meet its needs?" Each process, institution and practice is seen as performing a function that meets a societal need and thereby helps to maintain the society's structure or equilibrium' (1983:138). A more simple way to understand the basis of this perspective is to look at how it answers the seven basic questions highlighted by O'Donnell (1992).

1. How is society constructed?

Society is made up of various institutions which have specific purposes within society. These institutions perform certain functions which meet a need of that society, for example one of the functions of the family (which is a social institution) is the bearing and rearing of children. As societies develop the number and complexity of social institutions increase. According to O'Donnell, institutions can be grouped into four sub-systems:

(i)   economic (factories, offices)
(ii) political (political parties)
(iii) kinship (families)
(iv) cultural and community organisations (schools, churches). (1992:8)

2. How does society operate or function?

Functionalists consider that societies 'can be most easily understood and analysed if they are compared to biological organisms' (Marsh 2000:56). Social institutions work with one another for the benefit of society as a whole, for example schools function in relation to work because they prepare people for work. According to Bilton *et al.*, the education system performs three vital functions on behalf of society, that is, it 'helps to develop the human resources of an industrial nation . . . selects individuals according to their talents . . . and contributes to social cohesion by transmitting to new generations the central values of society' (2002:267).

3. Why are some groups in society more powerful than others?

Functionalists like Durkheim believe that it is necessary that some individuals and groups be more powerful than others, because only a limited number can make important decisions. Without leaders, society would descend into chaos.

4. What causes social change?

Functionalists believe that social change occurs when it is functionally necessary for it to do so. 'For example, in modern societies, educational systems tend to expand because such societies require a more literate and numerate population than less "advanced" societies' (O'Donnell 1992:8). Society adapts its norms to meet changing needs or to replace norms that have become dysfunctional. However, functionalists stress that change should be gradual because if it occurs too quickly it will result in confusion for members of that society.

5. Is society normally in orderly balance or in conflict?

Order is normal to society, but disorder can occur at times of war. Functionalists believe that order in society depends on the existence of 'moral consensus'. 'This means that everyone in society or nearly everyone shares the same values . . . For them, they stress the importance of the effective teaching of social values in maintaining order and conformity' (O'Donnell 1992:8).

6. What is the relationship of the individual to society?

The individual is formed by society through influences such as the family, school, religion, etc. Functionalists concentrate on how these institutions affect the individual.

7. What is the primary purpose of sociology?

The purpose of sociology is to analyse and explain the functioning of society.

Conflict theory: Marx

Marxism, like functionalism, concentrates on 'the structure of society and explains individual actions in terms of the social structure in which they are located' (Marsh 2000:61). However, while the functionalist approach is based on solidarity, this approach is based on division or inequality in society. Marx's work looked at conflict in society.

1. How is society constructed?

According to Marx, society is made up of classes. He believed that the system of capitalism produced two major classes. For him, a person's position in the class structure is determined by their relationship to the means of production. The most powerful class is the bourgeoisie – those who own the means of production, that is, land and factories. The proletariat are the least powerful class. This group does not own the means of production. Members of this group are forced to sell their labour (to the bourgeoisie) in order to make a living.

2. How does society operate or function?

Marx argued that in capitalist society, the bourgeoisie and the proletariat are opposed. In his view society operates mainly through class and conflict. He used the term 'class conflict' to refer to conflict between entire classes over the distribution of wealth and power in society.

3. Why are some groups in society more powerful than others?

Some classes are more powerful than others because they own more property and wealth. This power gives them the means to defend and keep what they hold.

4. What causes social change?

Social change occurs as a result of class conflict.

5. Is society normally in orderly balance or in conflict?

Marx concluded that societies throughout history have largely been characterised by conflict. While he did recognise that periods of social order can occur, they tended to benefit the rich and powerful more than others.

6. What is the relationship of the individual to society?

According to O'Donnell (1992), there are two major schools of thought amongst Marxists about the relationship of an individual to society:

- One school of thought sees the individual as powerless to affect their own life or that of others.
- The second school sees the individual having a much greater role in society.

7. What is the primary purpose of sociology?

The primary purpose of sociology is to describe, analyse and explain class conflict.

Social action theory: Weber

Max Weber (1864–1920), a German sociologist, was the founder of the social action perspective. Macionis and Plummer define this perspective as 'a micro theory that focuses on how actors assemble social meanings' (2002:26). Weber was more interested in the way people behaved and in how their behaviour influenced the wider society, as well as in social structure. 'Social action lies at the heart of the sociological approach, and only by understanding the intentions, ideas, values and beliefs that motivate people can you really know anything' (Osborne and Loon 1999:56). It was Weber's focus on social interaction in specific situations that resulted in his approach being considered as a micro-level orientation. Macro-level orientations, which means 'a focus on broad social structures that characterise a society as a whole' (Macionis and Plummer 2002:26), were shared by both the functionalist and conflict perspectives.

1. How is society constructed?

For Weber society is created through social interaction which involves people consciously relating to one another. People form institutions such as families and factories as a result of the process of interaction. Although people create institutions, institutions also influence people.

2. How does society operate or function?

Weber believed that individuals influence society and society influences the individual. People's ideas and feelings can inspire action in society but these actions are limited by the society they live in.

3. Why are some groups in society more powerful than others?

Weber agreed with the functionalists when he said it was necessary for some groups to have more power to ensure society functioned more efficiently. But he also accepted Marx's idea that those groups who do gain power in society use it primarily to protect their own interests

4. What causes social change?

Social change can occur for several reasons. 'Ideas, new inventions, war, the rise and fall of power groups, influential individuals and other factors all contribute to, and are part of, historical change' (O'Donnell 1992:11).

5. Is society normally in orderly balance or in conflict?
Weber considered that society is not normally either in balance or in conflict. He believed the state of society varies from case to case.

6. What is the relationship of the individual to society?
According to O'Donnell, Weber found it 'more important to understand the meanings that individuals experience in their own social lives than simply to analyse what 'causes' or 'influences' them to act as they do' (1992:12).

7. What is the primary purpose of sociology?
The purpose of sociology is to understand and explain the meaning of social action and interaction.

Feminism

According to Ahmed *et al.* (cited in Marsh 2002:257), 'Feminism is not one set of struggles: it has mobilised different women in different times and places, who are all seeking transformations, but who are not necessarily seeking the same thing, nor even necessarily responding to the same situation.' While there is no single theory of feminism, while it does not fit neatly into one particular strand, 'a set of recurring themes and principles does emerge . . . which are of particular importance to feminist practice' (Kelly 1988, cited in Marsh 2000:162). Those listed are:

(i)   the centrality of women's experience
(ii) research for women
(iii) the rejection of hierarchy and empowerment
(iv) the critical reflexivity.

Feminism can be defined as being a critique of society based on the inequalities that exist through gender roles and assumptions. Feminism does not see women being treated equally in terms of access to education, jobs, incomes, politics and power. According to Osborne and Loon, 'the programme that feminism would advocate for a reconstructed sociology would look something like this . . .

(i)   placing gender at the heart of all analysis, on a par with class and race
(ii) criticising all sociological theory for its male perspectives . . .
(iii) analysing the relationship between the public and private spheres as
      being of central importance in understanding how society functions
(iv) overhauling all of sociological theory' (1999:122).

Because feminism is in a constant state of development and because it encompasses so many different strands, such as liberal feminism, radical feminism, etc., it is difficult to pin down. According to Bell Hooks it 'is best described as a theory in the making' (cited in Marsh 2002:258).

SOCIOLOGICAL THEORY: STRUCTURAL PERSPECTIVES

Auguste Comte (1798–1857)
Emile Durkheim (1858–1917) → Functionalism
Karl Marx (1818–83) → Marxism/Conflict Theory
Max Weber (1864–1920) → Social Action Theory

EMILE DURKHEIM (1858–1917)

One of the great names of sociology was Emile Durkheim, a French sociologist who lived during the nineteenth century. At that time in Europe, huge changes accelerated by the Industrial Revolution were underway. Transformations were occurring in the way people lived their lives, how they organised their work, etc. Durkheim wanted to examine these changes and to try and understand what was happening. He wanted to understand how society functioned. Durkheim introduced the concepts of mechanical and organic solidarity and hence made a major contribution to the discipline of sociology. Areas that will be discussed in relation to Durkheim include:

- mechanical and organic solidarity
- anomie
- division of labour
- suicide
- religion.

Mechanical and organic solidarity

Durkheim developed an approach to help him try to understand society based on 'solidarity' and the different forms it takes. He argued that in pre-industrial societies, people were held together by a strong tradition (customs, values, etc.) which acted like a 'social glue' and held everyone in that society together. He believed the system in operation in those societies was '*Mechanical Solidarity* – meaning social bonds based on shared morality that unite members of pre-industrial societies' (Giddens 2001:9). This solidarity comes from likeness and similarity and has been described as being mechanical because people feel a more or less automatic sense of belonging together. Durkheim believed that in such small-scale societies people developed a *collective conscience* because they identified so much with other people in their community. Such a conscience would also allow them to punish anyone who challenged their way of life.

The advent of the Industrial Revolution meant the introduction of new machines, steam power, new ways in the production and transport of goods. Such developments brought huge changes to people's livelihoods and in the way work was organised. They also had a huge impact on the collective conscience of the group. As society became more complex due to an increase in the division of labour in society, mechanical solidarity began to break down and was replaced by a new type of solidarity: *organic solidarity*. This differed from mechanical solidarity in that where people had once seen unity in likeness, solidarity was now based on differences among people. This type of solidarity emerged from the division of labour which now required each worker to specialise in a single activity that had to be complemented by other specialised workers. Social bonds were based on the fact that people now relied on others who followed specialised pursuits; they were dependent on them in order to secure the goals and services they needed every day.

Organic solidarity was a characteristic of industrial or modern societies. People now were dependent on the efforts of people they didn't know. Specialisation or the division of labour meant that the foundation of traditional society, that is, moral consensus (moral agreement) was being replaced by functional interdependence. The emergence of industrial society in Europe in the nineteenth century did not extend equal rights to all its citizens. Such inequalities meant that some individuals and groups had restricted opportunities and unacceptable lifestyles. Instead of feeling a sense of unity or solidarity these people or groups experienced a sense of isolation or normlessness, what Durkheim termed Anomie.

Anomie

Durkheim believed that the social isolation or sense of meaninglessness associated with Anomie occurred when society didn't make an adequate transition from mechanical to organic solidarity. He believed that the division of labour progressed at a far greater extent than the moral guidance people required to live in a more free modern society. People did not have a clear idea of what is and what is not proper and acceptable behaviour. Individuals who experience anomie are not faced with sufficient moral constraint and hence feel isolated or meaningless. These feelings can impinge on their lives and their work. He also believed that such feelings can lead to suicide. 'As a society becomes more anomic, the suicide rate increases' (Mann 1983:12).

PRE-INDUSTRIAL SOCIETY
(primitive and traditional society)

▼

Low division of labour

▼

Collective conscience

▼

MECHANICAL SOLIDARITY

▼

Moral consensus

INDUSTRIAL SOCIETY
(modern society)

▼

High division of labour

▼

Moral individualism

▼

ORGANIC SOLIDARITY

▼

Functional interdependence

Division of labour

This is a very important term in sociology. Durkheim believed that many of the changes that came with industrialisation were a result of the division of labour in society. This concept refers to how work is organised. 'How tasks are divided and shared among the working population' (Tovey and Share 2000:9). Durkheim argued that in pre-industrial societies which had a low division of labour, one worker or work group (such as the family) did a range of different work tasks necessary to meet survival needs. Work was organised so that each stage in the production process was completed before the next was begun. This allowed a single worker to see the whole process through from beginning to end and to have a wide range of skills with limited specialisation. Modern society was characterised by a much greater division of labour. For Durkheim, 'the division of labour in society is a material social fact that involves the degree to which tasks or responsibilities are specialised' (Ritzer 1992:80). Ritzer goes on to say that 'People in primitive societies tend to occupy very general positions in which they perform a wide variety of tasks and handle a large number of responsibilities. In other words, a primitive person tended to be a jack-of-all-trades. In contrast, those who live in more modern societies occupy more specialised positions and have a much narrower range of tasks and responsibilities' (1992:80–81). According to Durkheim, this division of labour was more than just economic. Because work had become separate from the home and was extending rapidly into all areas of social life, a social division of labour was occurring. 'It is this wider fragmentation, this social division of labour, which has changed the relation of the individual to the moral order' (Lee and Newby 1986:216).

Suicide

In his famous work on suicide (1897), Durkheim 'attempted to link the personal act of suicide with the social forces in operation which might encourage it' (IPA 1992:9). By comparing statistics from different societies, he analysed them in terms of categories such as age, sex, religion and family relationships. From the evidence available he found 'that men, protestants, wealthy people and the unmarried each had significantly higher suicide rates compared to women, Roman Catholics and Jews, the poor and married people' (Macionis and Plummer 1997:6). He believed that such differences between groups corresponded to people's degree of social integration or strength of social ties. His work also highlighted the importance of social regulation in affecting suicide rates. According to Giddens, 'Durkheim identified four types of suicide in accordance with the relative presence or absence of integration and regulation' (2001:10–11):

1. egotistic suicide – too little integration
2. anomic suicide – too little regulation
3. altruistic suicide – too much integration
4. fatalistic suicide – too much regulation.

Egotistic suicide (too little integration): This occurs when there is insufficient integration in society. This type of suicide can occur when an individual feels isolated or when their ties to a group are weakened or broken. The extent of this suicide type can be shown by providing evidence of how suicide rates vary according to religion, marital status, etc.

Anomic suicide (too little regulation): This is a modern type of suicide and is a result of inadequate social regulation. This type of suicide can occur when people feel lost or isolated, feel like they don't belong. It relates to Durkheim's concept of anomie, which means that people are without the norms or rules to guide them in their everyday life.

Altruistic suicide (too much integration): This type of suicide is a characteristic of traditional and primitive societies where mechanical solidarity prevails. It is said to occur when an individual is over-integrated and values the society in which they live as more important than themselves. This type of suicide is found in the modern military context. Islamic suicide bombers are another example.

Fatalistic suicide (too much regulation): This type of suicide is a product of too much regulation and control and, for example, can be a characteristic of slave societies.

Durkheim believed that social factors could force an individual to take their own life when the state of society was not in orderly balance. According to Lee and Newby, 'The state of balance is defined in terms of two dimensions, i.e.

1. Integration: the extent to which individuals experience a sense of belonging to the collectivity.
2. Regulation: the extent to which the actions and desires of individuals are kept in check by moral values' (1986:223).

Different levels of the different types of suicide will be found in societies that display too much or too little of both integration and regulation.

Religion

Durkheim defined religion as 'a unified system of beliefs and practices relative to sacred things set apart and forbidden' (Selfe and Starbuck 1998:27). He saw religion as a necessary and essential feature of society. 'Religion served to integrate society together, produced shared values, justified the social order, produced opportunities for emotional expression, and gave an identity to individuals and groups' (Thompson 1986:4).

SUICIDE TYPES AND THE BALANCE OF SOCIETY

Excessive integration ⇒ (type of suicide: Altruistic)
Excess regulation ⇒ (type of suicide: Fatalistic)
Insufficient regulation ⇒ (type of suicide: Anomic)
Insufficient integration ⇒ (type of suicide: Egotistic)

(Source: Lee and Newby 1986:224)

According to Durkheim, the functions of religion include:

1. stability and cohesion
2. social identity
3. collective conscience
4. socialisation and social control
5. meaning and purpose. (Selfe and Starbuck 1998:27)

KARL MARX (1818–83)

Marx spent most of his adult life in London and while living there witnessed the growth of factories and industrial production. Although societies were producing more goods than ever before, he was awed by the inequalities that persisted between segments of society. Capitalism, an economic system 'which involves the production of goods and services sold to a wide range of consumers' (Giddens 2001:11) was dividing the population into two major classes:

1. the bourgeoisie – owners of property, factories, and
2. the proletariat – people who provide labour necessary to operate factories and other productive enterprises.

Marx used the term 'class conflict' to refer to conflict between entire classes over the distribution of wealth and power in society. 'Although owners of capital and workers are each dependent on the other – the capitalists need labour and the workers need wages – the dependency is highly unbalanced. The relationship between classes is an exploitative one since workers have little or no control over their labour and employees are able to generate profit by appropriating the product of workers' labour' (Giddens 2001:12).

Marx believed that the working class would become conscious of their exploitation (develop a class consciousness) and as a result they would act to produce social change which would bring about a fairer society. (Harvey *et al.* 2000:23)

Capitalism and alienation

Marx also criticised capitalism for producing alienation. He used the term to 'refer to the situation, whereby because of the unequal relationships of capitalism workers cannot achieve their full autonomy and potential' (IPA 1992:12). Alienation refers to the separation of individuals from themselves and others. 'At its simplest, alienation means that people are unable to find satisfaction and fulfilment in performing their labour or in the products of their labour' (Haralambos and Holborn 2000:68).

Marx looked at four ways in which capitalism alienates workers:

1. alienation from the act of working – workers are denied a say in what they produce and how they produce it
2. alienation from the product of work
3. alienation from other workers
4. alienation from human potential. (Macionis and Plummer 1997:81)

MAX WEBER (1864–1920)

Weber developed an approach 'that social behaviour is best understood by examining the meaning which people as social actors place on events and ideas. People can establish and justify reasons for actions and so make sense of the world' (Selfe and Starbuck 1998:32).

The sociology of action

According to Weber pre-industrial societies cling to tradition while people in industrial-capitalist societies embrace rationality. Actions of people in traditional societies are guided by the past, by beliefs about what is considered right and proper, because that is the way it has always been done. People in modern society take a different view of the world. They have a new way of thinking, they tend to choose to think and act on the basis of present and future consequences. For example, people in industrial society evaluate jobs, schools, etc., in terms of what we put into them and what we expect to receive in return. Weber presents four types of action:

1. **Traditional action:** Action carried out under the influence of custom or habit. A great deal of everyday activity comes under this heading.
2. **Affective action:** The action of the individual is guided by emotions; for instance, it may involve seeking revenge.
3. **Value-rational action or Wertrational:** The individual follows strongly held values and morals. Behaviour is guided by ideals. It is rational action because it involves the setting of objectives to which the person orients his or her activities. (Giddens 2001:74)
4. **Technical-rational action or Zweckrational:** Here the individual rationally calculates the probable result of a given act on the attainment of a particular goal. (Lee and Newby 1986:176)

For Weber, whole societies could be characterised by these forms of action.

The Protestant ethic and the spirit of capitalism

Weber showed how different religious ethics led to different economic outcomes. He showed that some world religions were not suited to the development of capitalism. 'Buddhism, Hinduism, Islam and Catholicism did not develop the necessary economic rational values to promote skills in financial occupations in the way that Calvinistic Protestantism did' (Selfe and Starbuck 1998:32). In his work *The Protestant Ethic and the Spirit of Capitalism* (1904), Weber was not saying that capitalism was caused by the rise of Protestantism, but the beliefs it provided were significant contributory factors. Calvinism did not teach that people must stay in the social class into which they are born. According to Weber, Calvinists approached life in a highly disciplined and rational way. He believed that industrial capitalism became established primarily in areas of Europe where Calvinism had a strong hold. The religious doctrine of John Calvin:

1. placed stress upon thrift and saving
2. encouraged reinvestment of capital into further economic activity
3. was based on a belief that it was divine will that the individual Christian should serve his God through hard work
4. stated that rewards from work matched effort expended. (Pryke 2002:133)

KEY FEATURES OF THE PROTESTANT ETHIC

The sovereignty of an all-powerful God who offers salvation.

▼

Predestination before birth, some form 'the elect'
who will be saved.

▼

But it is not known who the elect are. People must therefore
work for salvation to show they are worthy.

▼

Hard work becomes a virtuous activity, the sign of the good citizen
is the accumulation of great wealth.

▼

Salvation is the reward.

(Source: Selfe and Starbuck 1998:34)

Several movements have recently influenced the development of sociology. These include anti-racism, environmentalism and internationalism. These movements and their perspectives can be viewed as attempts to understand the developments that have taken place in society. 'Sociology has always sought to explain and make sense of change and is increasingly impelled to do so in the context of an interdependent world' (O'Donnell 1992:17).

4

Methods of Research and Social Investigation

CHAPTER OBJECTIVES

After reading this chapter you should be able to:

- define research
- distinguish between quantitative and qualitative methods, primary and secondary methods
- select and describe appropriate survey methods, e.g.
    - questionnaires
    - interviews – structured, semi-structured and unstructured
    - participant observation
    - experiment
    - secondary/historical analysis
- explain what is meant by 'sampling'
- write a report
- document and acknowledge sources consulted using the Harvard system of referencing.

RESEARCH DEFINED

Research can be defined as 'an attempt to increase available knowledge by the discovery of new facts through systematic scientific enquiry' (Clarke *et. al.* 2000:54). The idea of undertaking research may seem difficult or irrelevant to some students but once you become aware of the steps to be taken when carrying out a piece of research you can see how it contributes, by

1. attempting to resolve problems, and
2. helping us to understand why events happen as they do.

According to Hall and Hall, 'Research answers such questions as:

- What is happening?
- Why is that happening?

- How does that affect people?' (1996:10)

Students who engage in sociological research can investigate anything that is linked to society or people but before embarking on this 'journey of adventure, they must have a genuine interest in that area, an interest that will carry them through the research process' (Miller and Crabtree 1992:3, cited in Hall and Hall 1996:9).

Once an area has been selected for research, for example, Depression, you must then narrow it down to a specific topic. A simple way to do this is to ensure that your research topic statement has three points: a general area of study, a people point and a place point. So instead of having a broad subject area such as Depression, you would now have a more manageable topic, for example:

Depression among secondary school males in the Cavan area

Area under investigation	People point	Place point

It is important to remember that there are a number of factors at play when deciding on a topic for research. According to Scott (as cited in Marsh 2002:27), the three most important factors are:

1. Professional factors: How will the research meet the assessment criteria of a particular course?
2. Personal factors: How interested is the researcher in the topic?
3. Feasibility factors: How much time or money is needed to carry out the research?

Steps/stages in the research process

Define the problem: select a topic for research.
Review the literature: familiarise yourself with existing research on the topic.
Formulate a hypothesis: what do you intend to test?
Select a research design: choose one or more research methods – experiment, survey, observation, etc.

Carry out the research: collect your data, record information.
Interpret your results
Report the research findings: what is their significance? How do they relate to previous findings? (Giddens 2001:643)

Review the literature

Having selected a topic for research, the next step in the process is usually to review the available literature in the field. This is a very important part of the research process because researchers need to know what has already been written on their selected area. Carrying out a literature review allows the researcher to:

1. identify the gaps that exist in the literature available
2. see if previous research has identified a similar problem
3. see how other researchers have gone about resolving the problem.

A well conducted literature review could take several months or even years but it can provide invaluable information that adds to our knowledge base. Scott (cited in Marsh 2002:28), highlights that the main reasons for carrying out a literature review on the topic include:

- 'To avoid repeating work already done
- To try and build on existing work
- To seek out the gaps in the existing literature to produce something new and original
- To avoid repeating others' errors.'

Literature on a topic can originate from many sources, but for Benton *et al.*, (as cited in Cormack 2000:89), the following are the most common formats (see diagram). Some of these formats may be of greater value than others.

**SOURCES OF LITERATURE USED IN CONVEYING
RESEARCH INFORMATION**
Government circulars
Conference proceedings
Theses
Reports
Books
Journals
Computer databases/bulletin boards
(Source: Benton *et al.*, cited Cormack 2000:90)

Researchers must also be selective in the material they consult because of the huge volume of material available on all topics. To help ensure you gather relevant information and to make the task more manageable, Scott (cited in Marsh 2002:19) suggests you take some of the following steps:

1. See who are the key writers and theorists on your topic by looking through general introductory textbooks in the area.
2. Prepare keywords or phrases to use in catalogue and internet searches.
3. When reading the literature you should keep the following questions in mind and try to answer them:
   - Who is the author(s) of the piece of work, what is the title, date of publication, etc.? This information is needed when writing up your research.
   - What research methods were used to collect data?
   - What results did the research generate? What conclusions did the researcher draw?
   - How would you evaluate the research?

To carry out an effective literature review, researchers need to develop skills to enable them to assess what they are reading. They need to be able to identify the strengths and weaknesses of a piece of work and discuss its reliability and validity when applying it to a specific context. A good literature review depends on a researcher's skill in identifying these areas and then combining their views into a structured and logical review of the literature.

QUANTITATIVE AND QUALITATIVE METHODS, PRIMARY AND SECONDARY METHODS

Quantitative research: relates to quantity. 'It aims to study the relationship of one set of facts to another using scientific methods' (Donohoe and Gaynor 2003:281).

Qualitative research: relates to quality. This type of research seeks to gain understanding through the study of individuals.

In order for researchers to collect data in a systematic way, they need to employ a method. Methods of research include questionnaires, interviews, observation, etc. However methods are of two broad types:

'Primary methods involve researchers collecting their own data . . . The data they collect is "new" . . .', and
Secondary methods involve reanalysing information that 'has already been used as part of a research study' (Harvey *et al.* 2000:17).

A lot of research involves a mixture of primary and secondary methods.

QUESTIONNAIRES

Questionnaires are a primary method of data collection and are one of the most commonly used instruments for collecting information. The aim of the questionnaire is to gain information from the research population to enable the researcher to answer their overall research question.

'The ability of surveys to produce accurate data concerning behaviour, attitudes, conditions and opinions ensured that the survey became a central method within social science research' (Scott, cited in Marsh 2002:54).

However, despite its usefulness as a research instrument, careful consideration must be given to the preparation and design of the questionnaires. After all, answers obtained are only as good as the questions asked. The following is a list of some of the advantages and disadvantages associated with using questionnaires.

Advantages and disadvantages of questionnaires

Advantages

1. They can be distributed to large numbers of people.
2. They tend to be cheaper than other methods of data collection.
3. If designed properly, their analysis can be easier than other methods of data collection.
4. Persons completing the questionnaire can remain anonymous.
5. Administration is straightforward, especially when the questionnaire is distributed to a group or by post.

Disadvantages

1. There can be a low response rate.
2. Some people or groups may have difficulty or be unable to complete the questionnaire. For example the illiterate, young children, the visually impaired or non-native speakers may understand the spoken but not the written word.
3. The absence of an interviewer may mean it is impossible to clarify or rephrase certain questions.
4. There is a lack of personal contact between the researcher and the respondent. (Murphy-Black, cited in Cormack 2000:302)

Administration

Questionnaires can be administered in three different ways: postal surveys, face-to-face interviews and telephone surveys. Factors such as your research topic, time and travel will greatly influence the type you decide to use.

Designing a questionnaire

The design of a good questionnaire requires considerable preparation. Attention should be paid to the following:
1. What type of questionnaire are you going to use?
2. How long is the questionnaire going to be? (Researchers are generally advised to keep questionnaires short. By doing so it is hoped that they will maintain the interest and co-operation of the respondent.)
3. What types of question will you ask and how will questions be worded?
4. What format will questions take?

Types of question

There are a number of different types of question that can appear on questionnaires.

1. Closed question: This type of question requires the respondent to answer simply 'yes' or 'no'. They are not required to expand on answers. This may be seen as an advantage as it allows respondents to complete the questionnaire quickly, but it also means that individuals cannot offer any variation to their answers. An example of a closed question would be:

Have you studied sociology before?   Yes ☐ No ☐

2. Forced question: This type of question is very similar to a closed question in that answer categories are provided but they require more than a simple yes/no answer. The most commonly asked forced choice question to appear on questionnaires is that relating to gender, i.e.

Are you   Male ☐ Female ☐

3. Multiple choice question: This type of question provides the respondent with a list of possible answers and asks them to choose one or many from that list, for example:

Which of the following modules do you like studying? (please tick 2)

Applying psychology   ☐
Health promotion   ☐
Project   ☐
Social studies   ☐

With this type of question it is important to add 'Other, please specify' at the end in case you have omitted something from the list.

4. Ranking question: This type of question requests respondents to 'state their preference'. Researchers could provide respondents with a list of possible responses and ask them the following:

From this list of modules please rank according to usefulness to your work placement, where 1 is the most useful and 4 the least useful.

Applying sociology ☐
Equality, diversity and rights ☐
Care services ☐
Welfare rights ☐

Another way of approaching this type of question is to ask respondents to provide their own list and to rank them in order of importance, for example:

Please list the three modules you consider most useful to your course, with 1 being most useful and 3 least useful.

(1) _____

(2) _____

(3) _____

5. **Filter question**: This allows individuals who answer 'no' to a particular question to be directed to the next relevant question, for example

(1) Do you smoke   Yes   ☐
                       No   ☐

If No, go to question 5.

6. **Likert Scale**: This scale was devised by Likert in order to measure the attitudes and opinions of respondents. The main characteristic of this scale is that statements are provided and on the basis of a five-point scale respondents are asked whether they strongly agree, agree, neither agree nor disagree, disagree or strongly disagree, for example

	SA	A	NA/D	D	SD
All Irish people are racist	1	2	3	4	5

There are a number of important points to keep in mind when devising a Likert scale:

- Scales should consist of an equal number of positive and negative statements (this reduces researcher bias).
- Format of scales should ensure that negative and positive statements are adequately dispersed.

7. **Open question**: These questions allow respondents to give more detailed responses to questions, to comment in their own words and allow for individual variation. Researchers should provide enough space to allow respondents to do so. By leaving a number of lines etc., it also makes it clear

to the respondent exactly how much detail is requested from them, for example:

How do you feel about refugees in Ireland?

These questions can generate very useful information but too many of them in one questionnaire could deter a potential respondent. They are also more difficult to code and increase the work of analysis for the researcher.

Wording of questions

Careful consideration must also be given to the wording of questions. The general rule is to keep questions (1) short and (2) simple and straightforward. If questions are unclear, respondents may provide useless or irrelevant data that when collected will be of no benefit to the investigation. Use language appropriate to the population you are studying and when necessary define terms that need explanation. (Cormack 2000:304)

Questionnaire format

Attention to layout or format of a questionnaire is also very important. The following pointers will act as a guide to ensure your questionnaire is structured in a logical, coherent way.

1. **Title:** Always provide a title for your questionnaire.

2. **Introduction:** An introduction or an introductory letter is an important part of the questionnaire and should outline to the respondent the purpose of the study, provide information on the researcher and most importantly offer them a guarantee of confidentiality.

Sample introduction

My name is _____. I am a second year student in CCFS, studying for a BTEC Diploma in Social Care. As part of the course we are required to undertake a piece of research on a topic of our choice. The topic I plan to investigate is 'Discrimination experienced by members of the Travelling Community in Cavan town'. Your name has been selected as one of a simple random sample. The information you provide will be treated in the strictest of confidence. The questionnaire will take (approx.) 10–15 minutes to complete. Your help and co-operation is greatly appreciated. Thanking you . . .

3. **Instructions:** Researchers must give clear instructions on how to complete the questionnaire, i.e. tick boxes provided, circle numbers, etc.

If questions are not applicable, tell them to write N/A in the space provided.

4. **Question order:** According to Kane (1983:75), 'the usual practice is to place the questions in this order':

   (i)   broader, impersonal, easy-to-answer questions which enlist the respondent's co-operation and interest
   (ii) less interesting questions
   (iii) sensitive or personal questions, and open-ended questions.

Maintaining this order ensures that you are aware of your respondent's feelings and gives them a chance to ease into the questionnaire. (Kane 1983)

Problem questions

Kane in her work *Doing Your Own Research* (1983:78) points out a number of traps to avoid when writing your questions. These are as follows:

1. **The double question:** 'Do you cycle to college or have lunch in the canteen?' A question like this is confusing for the respondent as it contains two unrelated parts.

2. **The wrong choice question:** It is important to ensure that you give respondents appropriate questions and all the relevant choices of answers, for example, a question like 'Are you married, separated, divorced or widowed?' doesn't allow single people or people who never married a chance to reply.

3. **The kitchen sink question:** This question type asks several things in one question, for example 'Please list all the clubs you have joined in the past three years, activities taken, prices to join and reasons why you joined.' To ensure that a response will be in any way useful, ask each part of the question separately.

4. **The fuzzy-word question:** 'Should middle-aged people live it up?' There are two problems here, firstly 'middle-aged does not mean the same age group to everyone' (Kane 1983:78) and secondly living it up could mean anything from a fancy meal once a month to a night on the beer every week!

5. **The cover-the-world question:** 'What do you think of Bob Geldof?' A question like this could cause problems as it doesn't specify to the respondent what exactly they are to answer on, for example, are they to refer to his music, his work for Live Aid and Live 8 or to him personally?

6. **Dream questions:** What kind of job would you like for your child when

he or she finishes school? A question like this could produce hugely different responses from different individuals. For example, one parent might give an answer that states their absolute ideal, while another parent might provide an answer that is in line with their child's capabilities and talents.

7. **Leading questions:** Why are you happy in Cavan? This type of question assumes that people are happy in that area and doesn't give them the chance to say they are unhappy there if that is the case.

8. **Hearsay questions:** Avoid asking people the opinions of others. Asking the settled community about how Travellers feel about their new halting site does not provide an accurate picture of how the Traveller community actually does feel. (Kane 1983)

Other issues concerning questionnaires
1. Use good quality paper.
2. Use the same font size throughout.
3. Clearly number questions.
4. Provide enough space for answers.
5. Carefully code each question to facilitate the analysis process.

Pilot study

Having designed the questionnaire, the next stage in the process is a pilot study or what Robson refers to as a 'dummy run' (2002:383). 'The pilot study is a small version of the main study and is useful to test all the procedures and the feasibility of the study' (Murphy-Black, cited in Cormack 2000:311).

INTERVIEWS

'An interview is a series of questions a researcher addresses personally to respondents' (Macionis and Plummer 2002:50). This is also a primary method of data collection. There are many different types of interview, such as:

1. structured interview
2. semi-structured interview
3. unstructured interview.

The type you decide to use in your research will depend on the research topic, your research population, the kind of information you need, etc. You might find that your research topic might justify the use of all interview types.

1. Structured interview

With this type of interview you are asking each person the exact same question in the same order. The only difference between this and a questionnaire is that in an interview the researchers complete the form for the respondents as opposed to their doing so themselves, as they would with a questionnaire. It is a useful interview type to use when:

(i)   you are interviewing a large number of people

(ii)   you are interviewing people who share similar characteristics and outlooks

(iii) you have good background knowledge of your subject area, so that you know what is important to ask and how to ask it. (Kane 1983)

This type of interview produces quantitative data: information that can be neatly coded and analysed. This interview type does not leave much room for interviewees to expand on their answers or to offer variations on responses.

2. Semi-structured interview

Researchers who employ this interview type realise that it may take different questions, maybe put in a different order to get the same information from different people. For example, if you want to get attitudes on current childcare provision you must take into account that care providers, childcare workers and parents of those in childcare may focus on different aspects. The childcare provider may focus on government funding, the childcare worker on support services and the parent on quality of service.

This interview type may be more difficult or time-consuming to code as the answers provided may not fall into such neat categories as in the structured interview.

3. Unstructured interview

This type of interview produces qualitative or in-depth data. Instead of approaching the interviewee with a set of questions, the interviewer has a list of topics which they want the respondent to talk about. During the interview, the interviewee uses this list or topic guide to phrase questions in any order they want, at a time when it suits. It is a useful technique to use at the beginning of a research project, when you know very little on the research topic or when you are looking for a more in-depth sense of what people are thinking or feeling. Because this interview is more like a conversation, the interviewer must be experienced in order to manage it and to ensure the respondent does not go off on a tangent.

Advantages and disadvantages of interviews

According to Clarke *et al.* (2000:266), the following are some of the advantages/disadvantages of interviews:

Advantages

1. The interviewer may get all the sample to respond to the questions.
2. The interviewer can ask the respondents to explain their answers.
3. The interviewer can see if the respondents understood the questions.

Disadvantages

1. They are time-consuming and may cost a lot if you have to pay the interviewers, travel distances to conduct interviews, etc.
2. It can be difficult to interpret the data.
3. Interviewers have to be trained.
4. Personal interviews may intrude unnecessarily into people's lives.

Interviewer skills/techniques

1. Introduce yourself to the interviewee and explain the purpose and nature of the study to the respondent. Explain how they came to be selected.
2. Guarantee anonymity and confidentiality if appropriate.
3. Keep your objective in mind and do not deviate too far in an unstructured situation.
4. Explain to the respondent or interviewee that they are free to interrupt or seek clarification when needed.
5. Use probes to generate information but be sensitive when doing so!
6. Ensure your tone of voice, manner, gestures, etc., do not suggest a particular response.
7. Do not judge respondents by expressing approval or disapproval during the interview.
8. Be aware that the environment where an interview takes place can influence the quality of the interview. Where possible make sure the location is free from distractions (e.g. radio) or interruptions (e.g. telephones). Because information provided can be of a sensitive nature, it is important that interviewees are in a place where they feel safe, for instance where they are free of the fear of being overheard.

9. Ask for permission to record the interview and explain why you wish to do so.

PARTICIPANT OBSERVATION

Participant observation is 'a method by which researchers systematically observe people while joining in their routine activities' (Macionis and Plummer 2002:51). Researchers who use this method do so in order to gain an inside look at social life in a wide variety of settings. These settings could range from a more informal setting such as a shop or a nightclub to observation carried out in a laboratory. With participant observation the researcher is required to become some kind of member of the observed group. The researchers themselves become the research instruments and unlike other research methods, participant observation may require the researcher to become immersed in the setting for weeks, months or even years. 'The proponents of participant observation argue that it provides a depth of insight and penetration into social settings which other methods cannot match' (Mann 1983:278). Participant observation tells you what people do in situations where you get an opportunity to observe. As Kane points out, 'Participant observation is a technique to use when you wish to learn from people's actions what they do, as opposed to what they say they do' (1983:54).

Role of observer

As the name Participation Observation suggests, the information the observer gets will depend on their ability to become a participant in a particular setting. Gaining an 'insider's look' depends on the observer – 'hanging out' with others, attempting to act, think and even feel the way they do' (Macionis and Plummer 2002:51). This job of participant observer is not an easy one; in order to ensure that valuable/useful data is produced 'the observer has to remain neutral while at the same time being closely involved with those being studied' (Marsh 2000:149). During the study, the researcher must maintain some distance as an 'observer'. To ensure worthwhile data is collected great sensitivity and personal skills are required from the observer, as is their ability to mentally step back to record field notes and eventually to make sense of action. These roles of 'insider' participant and 'outsider' observer can cause a number of problems for the researcher, for example:

1. It can place physical and emotional demands on them.
2. It can result in both roles becoming blurred, i.e. role of observer with role of participant, which according to Marsh can cause 'role crisis' (2002:44).

The above problems have resulted in participant observation being criticised as a research method. Questions have arisen regarding its validity, especially as a method of data collection. 'Observation research is part craft and part art. Anyone can observe, but it takes practice and careful planning to observe and record a scene accurately and then to analyse perceptively anything of significance that happened' (Clarke *et al.* 2000:256).

After you observe you still have to make sense of what you saw. Kane believes that this requires much more than the observation tells you. You may also need to know

1. how representative your observation is
2. how often this kind of thing occurs
3. what people say about it.

You may also need to know if they would behave differently if you or other observers were not present. (Kane 1983:53)

Kane believes that the role of researcher involves:

1. observing and hearing with as much attention to detail as possible
2. recording, to the extent that is humanly possible, everything you see and hear in a situation
3. making no judgments about what is significant or irrelevant
4. recording any questions or comments which you make in the course of an observation, because they may have affected the situation.

Use of participant observation

Participant observation can prove useful when:

1. working with small groups
2. activities are accessible to observers
3. your prime motivation is to find out what is going on
4. you are not short of time (Robson 2002:316).

Advantages and disadvantages of participant observation

According to O'Donnell, the following are some of the advantages and disadvantages of participant observation:

Advantages

1. Some groups may have a lifestyle which makes it difficult to study them in any other way.
2. Researcher can fully understand relationships within the group being studied and therefore can understand why people behave in a particular way (and appreciate their point of view).
3. It is possible to study everyday routines and spot factors which might not appear important to the group members and which would not occur to them to mention in other circumstances.
4. Unexpected factors may emerge which the researcher might not have thought of.
5. The observer may not influence the group's behaviour if unrecognised as a researcher.
6. It is possible to record non-verbal communication.

Disadvantages

1. It may be difficult to control personal bias.
2. The presence of the observer may influence the behaviour of the group.
3. It may be difficult to gain acceptance by the group being studied.
4. It may be difficult to record information as it occurs, and important details may be forgotten.
5. There may be legal or moral problems: for example, a delinquent group may expect behaviour which is either illegal or contrary to the values of the observer.
6. There may be ethical implications: for example, 'undercover' operations tend to require the observer to lie in order to maintain 'cover'.
7. Participant observation is very time-consuming; it can create problems of cost and disrupt the 'normal' lifestyle of the researcher. (O'Donnell 2002:14)

EXPERIMENTS

'An experiment can be defined as an attempt to test a hypothesis under highly controlled conditions established by an investigator' (Giddens 2001: 649). This method is rarely used by sociologists because it is impractical and can involve too great a restriction on human rights. For this method to work, the researcher needs to directly control the circumstances being studied. Despite its limitations in social research, this method is mentioned as 'its classic experimental design helps us to understand the logic of all research designs' (Clarke *et al.* 2000:262). The experiment is seen as a pure form of research, as it asks not just what happens but why. It is for reasons such as this that the experiment is treated as a model against which other designs can be evaluated.

Advantages of experiments
1. The experiment, because of its nature, can usually be repeated and as a result can build up a body of data.
2. Experimenter bias is reduced, making this method the most objective.

Disadvantage of experiments
This method is difficult to use by sociologists as it is difficult to select and keep two similar group contexts.

SECONDARY/HISTORICAL ANALYSIS
'Secondary data – data often in the form of official statistics or statistics from other printed sources that have not been generated by the present researcher' (Bilton *et al.* 2002:444). The sociologist who uses this research method does not collect their own data personally, instead they use data collected by others. 'Secondary sources of information are records made or collected by others, and over a wide range of material' (Hall and Hall 1996:212).

These sources may include:
1. official statistics
2. published studies
3. other people's diaries and personal documents
4. public records
5. mass media reports
6. books
7. electronic media. (O'Donnell 2002:13)

Advantages of secondary research
1. Secondary research is cheap to use.
2. It may be more quickly available than primary sources.
3. It usually exists in considerable quantities.
4. It allows historical research.
5. It allows the researcher to compare one period with another.

Disadvantages of secondary research
Despite its advantages, secondary research has inherent problems, for example:

1. The data available may not exist in the form one might wish.
2. There could be problems with the accuracy of work done by others.
3. How objective is it? It can be difficult to account for researcher bias.
4. You may not be able to check the purpose for which it was originally collected.

Before you use secondary sources you must evaluate how reliable the information contained in it is. To enable you to do so Clarke *et al.* (2000:273) recommend that you should ask the following:

1. Who collected the data?
2. For what purpose was the data collected?
3. How was it collected?
4. Was the sample size large enough for the results to apply to your research?

Table 4:1 Four classic research methods: a summary

Method	Application	Advantages	Limitations
1. Experiment	For explanatory research that specifies relationships among variables, generates quantitative data.	Provides greatest ability to specify cause and effect relationships; replication of research is relatively easy.	Laboratory settings have artificial quality unless research environment is carefully controlled.
2. Survey	For gathering information about issues that cannot be directly observed, such as attitudes and values; useful for descriptive and explanatory research, generates qualitative or quantitative data.	Sampling allows surveys of large populations using questionnaires, interviews. Provides in-depth response.	Questionnaires must be carefully prepared and may produce a low return rate. Interviews are expensive and time consuming.

Method	Application	Advantages	Limitations
3. Participant Observation	For exploratory and descriptive study of people in a natural setting. Generates qualitative data.	Allows study of natural behaviour, usually inexpensive.	Time consuming. Replication of research is difficult. Researcher must balance roles of observer and participant.
4. Secondary Analysis	For exploratory, descriptive or explanatory research whenever suitable data is available.	Saves time and expense of data collection, makes historical research possible.	Researcher has no control over possible bias in data. Data may not be suitable for current research needs.

(Source: Macionis and Plummer 2002:52)

SAMPLING

'A sample: the numbers of people/groups about whom facts are gathered' (Donohoe and Gaynor 2003:282).

The term population refers to all those people that researchers have singled out for study. 'The term "population" is used here in a restricted sense, not of the population of a country but all the individuals who fall into the category of interest' (de Vaus 1991:60, cited in Hall and Hall 1996:106). These could be the employees of a factory or the students in a college, etc. Most surveys are of groups too large for everyone to be questioned individually. Because of this, researchers must select or 'sample' some individuals for questioning rather than others. According to O'Donnell (2002:18), researchers should ensure that:

1. the numbers are large enough to fairly represent the group
2. the number selected are reasonably easy and economic to handle.

'A sample is a portion of the universe and, ideally, it reflects with reasonable accuracy the opinions, attitudes or behaviour of the entire group' (Kane 1983:90).

One key problem for the researcher with taking a sample is making it representative. 'Sampling is essentially the process of selecting people or information to represent a wider population' (Marsh 2000:143). In order to ensure that the sample is representative, sociologists 'Incorporate a system of randomness into the selection procedure' (Cormack 2000:26). For Cormack, 'The term random does not mean haphazard or careless but refers to a precise method of selection where all individuals in a defined population stand an equal chance of being selected for inclusion in the study sample' (2000:26).

Different methods of sampling are available to the sociologist, including probability (or random samples) and non-probability (or purposive samples).

The most common types of sampling are:

1. **Random or probability sampling**, which includes
   (i)   simple random sampling
   (ii) quasi-random sampling (systematic sampling)
   (iii) stratified sampling
   (iv) multi-stage cluster sampling.

2. **Purposive or non-probability sampling**, which includes
   (i)   quota sampling
   (ii) snowball sampling
   (iii) judgmental sampling
   (iv) accidental or convenience sampling. (Hall 1996:109)

Probability sampling

1. Simple random sampling

With this sampling technique each member of the population has an equal chance of being selected for the sample. In order to use simple random sampling, you first need a list of all the people who could be selected (the sampling frame). The choice of who is actually included in the sample is made objectively by random means. Random numbers that are computer-generated can be used to select a sample. (de Vaus 1991:63, cited in Hall and Hall 1996:109)

2. Quasi-random sampling (systematic sampling)

This sampling method requires you to:

(i) firstly decide how many you want in your sample, and
(ii) then divide this number into the total in the sampling frame to give the sampling fraction.

For example, say you have a population of eighty and need a sample of ten. To calculate your sampling fraction divide eighty by ten; your sampling fraction would be eight (or the nearest whole number). Using a list of names or numbered items, pick the first name/item at random (say the second name on the list) and then every eighth name after that until ten are drawn. This is a fairly easy and cheap method but it is important to make sure lists themselves are not ordered or patterned in a way that could result in certain groups being overlooked. (Kane 1983:92)

3. Stratified random sampling

This sampling type requires you to order the population into different groups or strata, such as gender, age and social class, and then select information randomly within each stratum, usually by quasi-random sampling. For example, if you were studying the job concerns of all the employees within a VEC, the teachers, admin. staff, cleaners, etc., might have very different needs and interests. These groups could also differ very much in size. So in this method, you first divide the employees into strata (four in this case) and take a random sample from each stratum. The numbers in the strata are drawn to reflect their proportions in the study population. Thus, if our employees fell into the following numbers:

Teachers	80
Principals	20
Admin. staff	80
Cleaners	20
	200

We see that the teachers represents forty per cent of the total number, so in the sample they will also form forty per cent. If our sample is going to be sixty people, we will need twenty-four teachers (forty per cent of sixty), six principals, twenty-four admin. staff and six cleaners. These are selected by random sampling within each group. (Kane 1983:92)

4. Multi-stage cluster sampling

This is a good method to use when you have a large area to cover. For example, if you wanted to study how people in a city might feel about a new law, it would be too difficult and expensive to assign every voter a number and start from there. Instead, this method would permit you to:

1. divide the city into appropriate areas or regions and draw a sample of areas, and
2. take each sample area selected and draw a sample of voters from each.

However, to ensure your sample is representative of the entire population, this sampling technique would require you to have a good knowledge of the area and to make sure that no group had been omitted from the study.

Non-probability sampling

1. Quota sampling

'Quota sampling – where interviewers are instructed to find people to interview who meet the target numbers for the relevant characteristics of gender, age and social class (the 'quota').' (Hall and Hall 1996:112)

This type of sampling is often used in taking public opinion polls and the final selection of informants is left in the hands of the interviewer. This technique is often questioned by social scientists because those interviewed are quite literally those who were available at the time, for example those in the street at that time. Such a method can exclude a large number of the population whose attitudes and behaviour could be quite different from those asked.

However as this technique may be the only choice available to you due to limited finances, time, etc., be sure to make this clear in your study. Try to make sure that your quota reflects the proportion of each group or category in the area selected, for example if two per cent of the study population are Travellers, two per cent of your sample should be Travellers.

Snowball sampling

Sometimes in research it is impossible to identify beforehand all those who might fall into your category of interest. A sampling frame or list of the population may not be available. For example if you were conducting research on deviance, you may not find accessible a list of 'deviants' who can be surveyed. In this situation, you can use snowball sampling where the researcher begins with one or a few contacts, who then help to find others, and so on. 'Like rolling a snowball, the sample gets bigger the more interviewing you do' (Hall and Hall 1996:113).

Judgmental sampling

This type of sampling is similar to quota sampling, but less detailed. According to Hall and Hall 'a judgment sample relies on the researcher to try to obtain as wide a representation of individuals as possible, taking account of likely sources of difference in their views and experiences' (1996:115).

Accidental or convenience sampling

This is a quick and cheap way of sampling that involves simply asking anyone who happens to be around and available. Because of this we do not know how representative the results are of the relevant population.

A good sample is not solely dependant on size. Researchers must also:

1. avoid bias in the selection procedure
2. aim to achieve maximum precision for the resources available.

'A poor sample can be disastrous – it can provide misleading information and result in errors' (Clarke *et al.* 2000:268).

WRITING A REPORT

Most research ends with the production of a text of some sort. It is this stage in the research process that can cause many problems for students. It is important to plan your work, to work through drafts and always to proofread them. The following checklist provided by Marsh acts as a guide for students writing up a piece of work. He believes the more 'yes' answers the more chance you have of your finished text being up to assessment standard.

Table 4:2 Writing Checklist

	YES (please ✓)	NO (please ✓)
1. Do I fully understand what I am being asked to do?		
2. Do I fully understand my assessment criteria?		
3. Do I have sufficient literature review?		
4. Do I need to include an abstract?		
5. Have I included transcripts if required?		
6. Do I need to include a discussion of timescale and planning?		
7. Do I need to include a discussion on budget?		
8. Have I reviewed methodological issues and shown where my research fits?		
9. Have I discussed my choice of research techniques fully and clearly?		
10. Is my data clearly presented?		

Writing Checklist (contd.)

	YES (please ✓)	NO (please ✓)
11. Have I discussed ethics?		
12. Do I analyse my data sensitively and as accurately as possible?		
13. Do I place my research and data in the wider sociological context?		
14. Do I offer suggestions for improving future research?		
15. Do I incorporate the work of others in my data analysis?		
16. Do I evaluate my research in relation to the work of others?		
17. Do I offer a critical awareness of my research?		
18. Do I have a clear and well-organised structure to the text?		
19. Are sentences short and snappy?		
20. Have I used subtitles and headings to make the text clearer?		
21. Do sectors link well together?		
22. Have I used the correct referencing system?		
23. Have I included a correctly constructed bibliography?		
24. Is it word-processed?		
25. Have I done a spell check?		
26. Have I read through a draft to check grammar and spelling?		
27. Have I asked someone else to read through a draft to check grammar and spelling?		

(Source: Marsh 2002:67)

There is no one way to organise a report. The following headings are provided as guidelines:

1. **Title:** The title of your report should summarise the main topic of the report. The title deserves considerable attention as it is that that 'sells' the

report. Your title can change during the course of the work; do not be afraid to change it. 'A two-part title structure is common: something capturing the essence of the study followed by a more descriptive subtitle' (Robson 2002:509). The title page should also include:

(i)   name of report writer
(ii) date of submission
(iii) organisation name (if appropriate).

2. Summary/abstract: A concise summary (typically 100–150 words) allows other readers to quickly see if the research is of interest to them before they read the main body. The summary or abstract should explain what you did, the methods you used and the results.

3. Introduction: This should provide the reader with a general description of the research problem. It should also:

(i)   explain why you undertook the work
(ii) state your hypothesis
(iii) state the aims of your research. (Clarke *et al.* 2000:302)

4. Review of literature: The purpose of the review is to inform the reader of relevant literature you have read directly relating to your research. The review should provide the reader with an overview of the field you are studying. It should also include:

(i)   an evaluation of this previous work
(ii) the relationship of your work to those earlier studies.

According to Cormack, 'Literature which is supportive of, and which disagrees with, the research being reported is also included' (2000:449).

5. Methodology: Robson in *Real World Research* lists the following as areas that need to be dealt with in the methodology chapter:

(i)   the kinds of data you have obtained
(ii)   why this data was selected
(iii) how the data was obtained including issues of access and consent
(iv)   the methods used to collect the data
(v)   why these methods were used
(vi)   the approach taken to data analysis
(vii) discussion of the reliability, validity and generalisability of the data
(viii) the decisions made during the course of the study, including change of focus and direction
(ix)   ethical issues raised by the study and the procedures followed to address them. (Robson 2002:510)

6. **Results:** This section gives you the opportunity to present your results. Collected data should be clearly described, analysed and presented. Tables, graphs etc., can be used to present data.

7. **Analysis and discussion:** 'The discussion will enable speculation about the meaning of the findings, recognition of the limitations of the study and suggestions for future research in the subject area' (Cormack 2000:451). This section enables you to discuss to what extent your results support or do not support your original hypothesis. Do not introduce new research data in this section.

8. **Conclusions:** The major aim of the closing section, according to Donohoe and Gaynor, is 'Summarise, clarify, evaluate and recommend' (2003:287). Present any conclusions you have drawn from your results and on the basis of these make recommendations.

9. **Appendices:** In this section include material that is not suitable for the main part of your study, for example newspaper cuttings, maps, a copy of any questionnaire you issued, etc. It is important to label them clearly so that the reader can refer to them in the main text. The last few pages of your appendices should be your bibliography, a detailed list of all the references and sources you have used in your report.

Presentation and organisation of a report

1. Use language that is clear and understandable.
2. Be honest and accurate.
3. Organise the parts of the paper. According to Kane, a paper may have any of the following:

Table 4:3

Preliminary material	Main body	Reference materials
1. Title	7. Introduction	12. Appendix
2. Abstract	8. Methodology	13. Footnotes
3. Preface	9. (The paper proper)	14. Glossary
4. Table of contents	10. Conclusions	15. Bibliography
5. List of tables	11. Suggestions for Future Research	16. Index
6. List of illustrations (pictures, charts, diagrams, maps, etc.)		

(Source: Kane 1983:177-178)

THE HARVARD SYSTEM OF REFERENCING

Why reference?

'It is to acknowledge the work of other writers, to demonstrate the body of knowledge on which you have based your work, to enable other researchers to trace your sources and lead them on to further information' (www.Imu.ac.uk).

A number of referencing systems are used by researchers when acknowledging the work of authors, for example the Harvard system and the footnote system.

According to Cormack, the Harvard system of referencing is 'perhaps the most widely used system for citing references within scientific publications' (2000:110). When you use this system you cite the surname of the author and the year of publication of the work within parentheses. If readers need to find out more information regarding the material being cited such as the title of the work, the name of the publishing company, etc., they must consult the bibliography at the end of your report. This is an alphabetically ordered list of all the references you have used in your work. References are organised alphabetically according to author's surname.

The Harvard system: According to the web page www.LMU.ac.uk, the Harvard system was developed in the USA in the 1950s and 60s and has 'become the most common system internationally'. It is considered a flexible, simple, clear and easy to use system for both reader and author. Donohoe and Gaynor (2003:291) highlight the following points that a researcher should follow when referencing work:

1. Quotations must be taken word for word from the original text.
2. Quotations of three lines or less should begin and end with a single inverted coma (quotation mark).
3. When quotations are longer than three lines, omit quotation marks and indent the quotation. Along with author's surname and year of publication of the work, give the page number, so that the reader can check the accuracy of the statement, for example (Walsh 2004:10).
4. If you do not quote a sentence in full you indicate this by use of an ellipsis, i.e. . . . .
5. When there are multiple authors, only cite one followed by 'et al.' meaning 'and others'.

Bibliography: list of references

A bibliography is an alphabetically ordered list of the references you have referred to in the body of your work. When arranging this list there is no need to separate books from journals or any other type of material. However, it is important that you provide the following information when referring to:

Books

1. Author(s), editor(s) or the institution responsible for writing the document
2. Year of publication in brackets
3. Title (and subtitle) underlined
4. Series and volume no. (if applicable)
5. Edition (if not the first)
6. Publisher
7. Place of publication.

For example:

Kane, E. (1983) <u>Doing Your Own Research</u>, Turoe Press Ltd, Dublin.

Journal articles

1. Author's surname followed by initials
2. Year of publication in brackets
3. Title of article in quotes
4. Title of journal (underlined)
5. Volume and part number, month or season of the year
6. Page numbers of article.

For example:

Gaffney, C. (2003) 'Social Research', <u>Irish Journal of Sociology</u> No. 3, Spring, pp. 90–95.

If the article is anonymous:

Social Research? (2003) <u>Irish Journal of Sociology</u> No. 3, Spring, pp. 90–95.

Edited collections or 'In' references

1. Author's surname, followed by initials (of chapter/section)
2. Year of publication in brackets
3. Title of essay or chapter, 'in' followed by colon
4. Author or editor of collected work
5. Title of collected work (underlined)
6. Publisher

7. Place of publication
8. Page numbers of section referred to.

For example:

Kelly, M. (2004) 'Women in Ireland' in: Sweeney M., ed. <u>Feminism in Ireland</u>, Gill and Macmillan, Dublin, pp. 66–71.

Newspaper articles
1. Author of article
2. Year of publication in brackets
3. Title of article
4. Title of newspaper (underlined)
5. Date of publication
6. Page number(s) of article.

For example:

McDonald, D. (2004) 'Rise in Crime Rate' says report, <u>The Anglo-Celt</u>, 15 September, p. 3.

Theses and dissertations
1. Author's name
2. Year of publication (in brackets)
3. Title (and subtitle if any) underlined
4. Type of document (e.g. M.A., Ph.D, etc.)
5. Place of publication
6. Awarding institution.

For example:

Elsadig, O. (2004) <u>Ethics in Research</u>, Ph.D thesis, University College Dublin.

Film
1. Film title (underlined)
2. Date of release (in brackets)
3. Director's name
4. Place of publication
5. Production company name
6. Medium: format in square brackets [].

For example:

<u>Dreams</u> (2002) Directed by Ciara Gaffney. New York, Warner [Film: 35 mm]

Video/documentary
1. Series title
2. Year
3. Programme title (underlined)
4. Place of publication
5. Publisher
6. Date of transmission
7. Medium: format in square brackets [].

For example:

Questions and Answers. (2000) <u>Crime rates in Ireland</u>. Dublin, RTE, 2 March [Video:VHS]

(Adapted from web page www.LMU.ac.uk: pp 7–15)

Electronic journal articles
1. Author(s)/editor(s)
2. Year
3. Title of article
4. Title of journal (underlined)
5. Type of medium
6. Date of publication
7. Volume no. (issue no.) pages, etc.
8. Availability statement
9. Date of access in square brackets [].

For example:

Walsh, P. (1999) Sociology in Ireland, <u>Journal of Sociology</u> [Internet] 5 March, 2 (4), pp. 122–4. Available from: <http://lmc.ac.irl> [Accessed 1 June 2001]

World Wide Web documents
1. Author/editor
2. Year
3. Title (underlined)
4. [Internet]
5. Edition
6. Place of publication
7. Publisher (if ascertainable)
8. Available from: <URL>
9. Date of access in square brackets [].

For example:

Smith, S. (2000) <u>Law Reform</u> [Internet] Dublin City University. Available

from: <http:///www.dublincity.ac.irl/service.depts_Pub.lawreform.html>
[accessed 22 July 2002]

Other issues concerning bibliographies
1. When a web page does not give an author, use the title as the main reference point as you would do with an anonymous work.
2. 'Second and subsequent authors' initials come before the surname' (Donohoe and Gaynor 2003:293).
3. The abbreviation 'ibid.' can be used when you refer to the same author and book twice (or more) in a row and when there is no other reference between them. Ibid. (ibidem) means 'the work referred to above' (Donohoe and Gaynor 2003:293).

5

Sociology of the Family

THE FAMILY DEFINED

'Any combination of two or more persons who are bound together by ties of mutual consent, birth and/or adoption or placement and who, together, assume responsibility for, *inter alia*, the care and maintenance of group members through procreation or adoption, the socialisation of children and the social control of members' (UN, cited in Donohoe and Gaynor 2003:242).

The family is regarded as one of the most basic and important institutions in society, because it is where society is reproduced in its most basic form, the individual. Defining 'family' is not simple as it takes many forms. 'There is no such thing as the family – only families' (Giddins 1993, cited in Macionis and Plummer 2002:436). Sociologists say that there is no such thing as the family, 'no single definition that can encompass the myriad of domestic and kinship arrangements that characterise contemporary social life' (Sclater 2000:6). The family is an area of great interest to sociologists especially when set in a comparative context over time and culture.

All societies contain some form of family arrangement. Several decades of research, inquiry and discussion have enabled sociologists to increase our understanding of the family, its changing patterns over time and its role within the wider society.

THE CHANGING FAMILY – RANGE AND CULTURAL DIVERSITY

The great diversity of family and household forms has become an everyday feature of our age. Family patterns have undergone rapid change over the past several decades. 'The major difference which engaged sociological research and debate concerns the transition from a predominantly extended family form in pre-industrial times to the nuclear or conjugal family more typical in modern industrial society' (IPA 1992:34). Sociologists have identified the following family types:

- **The extended family:** Consists of parent(s) and their children plus other relatives such as grandparents, aunts, uncles, etc. living with them or very close to each other. The Irish extended family was also referred to as the stem family. It usually consisted of two generations, the parents, the son and his wife and their children and his unmarried brothers and sisters. (IPA 1992:34)
- **The nuclear family:** Consists of two adults living together in a household with their own or adopted children. The nuclear family lives in a unit that is separate from the wider family. According to Donohoe and Gaynor (2003:247), this family type also includes one-parent families which consist of one parent and a child or children living together. One-parent families occur because the parent has never lived in a partnership or because of death, separation or divorce.
- **The reconstructed family or step-family:** Consists of two people who have had children in previous relationships and who are now married or live together and each bring their children to live together with the new children they may decide to have.

Families are linked by kin connections. Kinship ties are 'connections between individuals through marriage or through lines of descent that connect blood relatives' (Giddens 2001:173). Marriage can be defined as 'legally sanctioned relationships, involving economic cooperation as well as normative, sexual activity and child-bearing, that people expect to be enduring' (Macionis and Plummer 2002:436).

There are three basic ways in which a family may be constituted:

1. monogamy – one man married to one woman
2. polygyny – one man married to several women

3. polyandry – one woman married to several men. (O'Donnell 2002:36)

Polygamy is the term used to cover both polygyny and polyandry. Economic, social and sexual reasons influence the existence of any particular family pattern, for example in societies where polygyny is practised there are usually more girls than boys.

Table 5:1 Differing Family Patterns

Types	Examples
1. **Polygyny:** one man and more than one woman. Surplus of women, sometimes artificially increased by early marriage for girls and late marriage for men, or by acceptance of homosexuality. Also men more likely to be killed, i.e. war. (Note: only the rich and/or powerful may have more than one wife.)	Saudi Arabia, Masaí and Yoruloa in East Africa. (The Koran permits Moslem men to have up to four wives.)
2. **Polyandry:** one woman and more than one man. Surplus of men (rare). May be enforced in order to limit children born and reduce pressure on scarce resources.	Tibet, some Eskimos.
3. **Monogamy:** one man and one woman. Roughly equal balance between sexes. Tends to occur as hygiene and medical care reduce imbalance between sexes, (i.e. greater infant mortality among males) and/or modern wage economy makes additional wives/children economic liability rather than economic asset.	Modern Europe, USA.

(Source: adapted from O'Donnell 2002:41)

Families can also be classified by power and on lines of descent.

Power

Patriarchal
Wealth and power come from the father and he controls the family.

Matriarchal
Mother controls the family.

Egalitarian
Authority in the family is more or less equal.

Descent
Patrilineal
Descent through the father – takes father's surname, sons inherit.

Matrilineal
Descent through the mother.

Bilineal
Descent through both mother and father. (O'Donnell 2002:37)

Exogamous marriage permits individuals to marry someone from outside the group to which they belong. Endogamy on the other hand means that individuals are normally restricted to marrying someone of their own social group. (Haralambos and Holborn 2000:180)

PERSPECTIVES ON THE FAMILY

Functionalist perspective on the family

This approach believes that families perform vital functions for their members and for society. These functions include:

1. **Socialisation:** According to sociologist Talcott Parsons, the family's 'main functions are primary socialisation and personality stabilization' (Parsons and Bales 1956, cited in Giddens 2001:175). When children learn the cultural norms of the society into which they are born, the process is referred to as primary socialisation. Because this process happens during a child's early years, the family is considered a hugely important setting for the development of the human personality. For Giddens, 'Personality stabilisation refers to the role that the family plays in assisting adult family members emotionally' (2001:175).

2. **Regulation of sexual activity:** 'Every culture regulates sexual activity in the interest of maintaining kinship organisation and property rights. One universal regulation is the incest taboo, a cultural norm forbidding sexual relations or marriage between certain kin' (Macionis and Plummer 2002:440). Different societies have rules regarding who can marry who but they usually apply the incest taboo to close relatives. Apart from the fact that reproduction between close relatives could have negative affects on the

mental and physical health of offspring, Macionis and Plummer highlight the social reasons for the taboo:

(i)   It minimises sexual competition within families, by restricting sexual relations to spouses.

(ii) It forces people to marry outside their immediate families to form broader alliances.

(iii) It keeps kinship intact. (2002:440)

3. Social placement: A child's identity based on race, ethnicity, religion and social class is ascribed at birth through the family. Families permit the transmission of wealth and status from parents to children.

4. Material and emotional security: Family members are dependent on each other economically and emotionally. This was specially the case when there was no social welfare system and when the state did not provide support. According to Parsons, 'men performed an instrumental role, that of economic provider (or breadwinner) whilst women's role was an expressive one, as nurturer and emotional provider' (cited in Sclater 2000:220).

Criticisms of functionalist perspective

This perspective has been criticised for a number of reasons, as follows:

1. Children are socialised outside the traditional family.
2. People have sexual relations outside the family.
3. Increasing evidence of violence and abuse within families suggests that the family can be a dysfunctional place.
4. This perspective minimises the problems of family life.
5. Family plays a part in reproducing and maintaining the capitalist system.
6. This perspective pays little attention to how other social institutions meet some human needs.
7. The anti-psychiatry movement in the 1960s and 70s 'pointed to the demands and tensions of ordinary family life as instrumental in the production of mental illness' (Sclater 2000:25).

Class-based analysis of family: conflict theory

This perspective on the family views it as another institution that is involved in 'promoting dominant societal values and perpetuating the exploitation of subordinate groups by upholding the norms and values of capitalist society' (Marsh 2000:554).

Marx and Engels looked at the role of families in the social reproduction of inequality. The contribution of Marxism to the sociology of the family can be summarised in the following points:

1. Through the socialisation of children, the family reproduces both labour power and a false ideology which keeps the capitalist system going. 'Families thus support the concentration of wealth and reproduce the class structure in each succeeding generation' (Macionis and Plummer 2002:440).
2. Patriarchy: Engels stated that families transform women into the sexual and economic property of men. Women perform unpaid labour in the home that would otherwise cost a lot to those who benefit from it. By controlling the sexuality of women, men know who their heirs are. Women also make up a 'reserve army' of labour that can be called on, for instance in times of war.
3. Race and ethnicity: As people continue to marry others like themselves (endogamy), racial and ethnic categories will continue to persist.

Critical comments on conflict theory

This perspective has been criticised because though Engels condemned the family as part of capitalism, non-capitalist societies also have families and family problems.

Feminist approaches to the study of the family

Much research on the family, carried out in the 1970s and 1980s, was dominated by different feminist perspectives. In looking at the family they focused on the presence of unequal power relationships within the family and on showing that certain family members tend to benefit more than others. They argued that men generally benefit greatly from families whilst women often do not. 'Feminists highlight the continuing exploitation of women in capitalist societies, not least in terms of the way in which their contribution to the bulk of private domestic work remains unrecognised, unrewarded and undervalued labour' (Marsh 2000:552).

Feminists argue that within the family, the woman:

- has little decision-making autonomy
- has to do more housework than men, and still spends more time looking after the children, the sick and the elderly (Finch 1989, cited in Macionis and Plummer 2002:441).

Feminists claim that despite the fact that violence and abuse that occurs within some families has received much more public attention, problems such as 'wife battering, marital rape, sexual abuse of children, have long been ignored in both academic contexts and legal and policy circles' (Giddens 2001:177). For many feminists, 'the private isolated nuclear family is seen not as a functional unit, but as dysfunctional, particularly for women and children' (Sclater 2000:27). A feminist perspective has significance in the sociology of the family as it highlights:

1. the importance of women within the core of the domestic unit
2. the changing attitudes to and roles of women in the areas of marriage, divorce and cohabitation
3. the increasing significance of women's roles as carers within the community. (Marsh 2000:554)

A critic of this perspective suggests that feminists fail to take into account the growing trends towards equality in decision-making between women and men.

THE FAMILY STRUCTURE IN IRISH SOCIETY

'The family, in Ireland as elsewhere, has been identified as an important symbol of collective identity, unity and security' (O'Connor, cited in Tovey and Share 2003:89).

The nature and structure of the family unit in Ireland has undergone major changes over the years. 'As in other societies modernisation and industrialisation have had an enormous impact upon the traditional Irish family including family relationship patterns, kinship and the conjugal relationship itself' (IPA 1992:35). Two studies carried out by Arensberg and Kimball in the 1930s and Hannan in 1976 provide profiles of family life and family relations that are very different to each other and provide some evidence of the major changes that have occurred. The typical family described by Arensberg and Kimball was characterised by:

1. a strong localised community and kinship network
2. a domestic subsistence economy
3. clearly and sharply defined roles according to age, sex and relative status. These family roles were also work roles.

At the time of this study, the Irish traditional family was structured around the domestic economy of the farm and household. The family was seen primarily as a unit of production and reproduction. The success of this economy base required full commitment from family members and as a result rigid roles emerged that reflected the work roles of its individual members. The father's role was that of provider and as owner-director of the family farm he was the 'object of obedience and respect from his children and wife' (Ibid.:36). The wife/mother dominated within the household, as she was responsible for the care of the children, housekeeping duties and some areas of farm work. The clear distinction in the roles of husband and wife meant that family roles were more formal and lacked emotional depth. Arranged marriages or 'matchmaking' was also common in 1930s Ireland and was a matter for the couple's parents and kinsfolk. 'Marriage was essentially understood in terms of its role in transmitting property and creating new kin networks of co-operation' (IPA 1992:36). Hannan's 1976 survey of farm families found greater diversity in family relationships ranging from 'the rigidly traditional patterns to patterns more characteristic of modern urban middle class families' (*Ibid.*: 37). The results of his survey presented some of the following findings:

1. One-third of his sample displayed traditional sex roles and decision-making patterns similar to those of the traditional family in the 1930s. This pattern was reflected more in the older age groups.
2. One-quarter of the sample had what 'Hannan described as a very modern pattern of interaction involving joint decision-making, more sharing of tasks especially childcare tasks' (IPA 1992:37).

These families tended to be younger, not as socially isolated or embedded in their community. They had more contact outside of their own immediate community.

Despite change, Galligan (1998, cited in Tovey and Share 2003:244) states that 'At the same time the more limited notions of the "traditional" family continue to receive active support from many, if not the majority in Irish society. In particular, most men and women that are not working outside the home, tend to have more traditional views in relation to the family.' In modern society, the traditional functions of the family have been transferred to other social institutions, for example:

- Crèches, nurseries and pre-schools can provide full day care from the age of three months, and later on schools provide education.
- The social service system can provide children with the basic necessaries such as food, shelter, etc., should the need arise.

The following is evidence that reflects the shift in the structure of the family in Irish society today:

1. Relationships and marriages are driven on the 'relatively modern westernised notion of romantic love' (Donohoe and Gaynor 2003:243). This concept sees individuals as free to choose their own spouse. In traditional Irish society arranged marriages were common, and were organised by family members and other kin.
2. Births outside marriage are also on the increase. According to Tovey and

Share (2003:246) these births made up nearly a third of all births in Ireland. This increase reflects a change in attitudes about our ideas about the family and in social values. 'The introduction of the Unmarried Mother's Allowance in 1973 gave a means of supporting children outside of marriage without family approval or support' (Donohoe and Gaynor 2003:247). Despite economic assistance from the state, lone parents constitute a large number of the population who experience poverty and discrimination in society.

3. There has also been an increase in the number of one-parent families. Apart from people who never married or lived in a partnership, this group includes a parent on their own as a result of death, separation or divorce. Statistics provided by Donohoe and Gaynor (2003:247) reflected findings from the Central Statistics Office 1996. These showed that in 1996:
   - fifteen per cent of all family units in Ireland were lone parent families
   - four-fiths of these were headed by women
   - twenty-eight per cent of all lone-parent families in Ireland were resulting from separation or divorce.

Other features of the family in Irish society include:
- a decline in the marriage rate (in the Republic of Ireland the total number of people getting married fell from a high of 22,180 couples in 1980 to 17,360 in 1995)
- later age in marriage and first childbirth
- smaller completed family size (1981–96: families with one and two children grew by twenty-six per cent and thirty-four per cent respectively (www.family.com)
- an increase in the number of people remaining single. (Tovey and Share 2003:245)

Major changes in the family can be attributed to factors such as the modernisation of Irish society, a decrease in the adherence to religious regulations, changing attitudes of women, etc. 'Ireland, like many other western countries, has seen a major change in the nature and structure of the family unit in recent times' (*Ibid.* 2003:245).

Divorce in Ireland

Divorce was introduced to Ireland by the Family Law (Divorce) Act, which came into force on 27 February 1997 (Wood and O'Shea 2003:65). In 1995 Ireland was the only country in the European Union to forbid civil divorce.

In November 1996 the electorate in Ireland voted in favour of divorce, 818,842 votes to 819,728, after a recount (Wood and O'Shea 1997:15).

Divorce is seen as the last option by a couple when their marriage breaks down and can have a traumatic effect on all those involved, including the couple, any children, and society as a whole. Despite this, divorce is a realistic and accepted part of life in twenty-first-century Ireland. The following statistics support this fact:

- Between February 1997 and December 2001, 10,182 divorces were granted in the Circuit Court.
- A further eighty-three divorces were granted in the High Court.
- Between 1990 and 2000 the number of District Court applications (in family law matters) for divorce rose from 8,028 to 23,452.
- In the year 2001 almost 3,500 applications for divorce were received by Circuit Courts around the country.
- Over sixty per cent of those applying for divorce were women. (Wood and O'Shea 2003:65)

FAMILY DISINTEGRATION AND BREAKDOWN: PATTERNS AND REASONS

Violence

'The true numbers of violent episodes that occur in homes up and down the country, as it remains is a largely a "hidden problem", taking place behind closed doors, often with no witnesses present' (Sclater 2000:104). According to Donohoe and Gaynor, 'domestic violence refers to violence in the home perpetrated by adults on their partners and/or children' (2003:245). It was only in the 1970s that violence against women and children was recognised as a social problem. Despite the discovery of this new 'family problem' it is still difficult to estimate the true extent of it, as many feel it is difficult to report (Macionis and Plummer 2002:445). Domestic violence occurs across all social classes and includes physical and sexual assault. Men can also be the victims of domestic violence, however the majority of studies document the violence experienced by women. Evidence provided to support this shows that:

- Twelve barring orders a week are granted against violent partners in Dublin. (The majority of these are against men.)
- Sixty-five women were murdered in Ireland between 1996 and 2002. One-third of these were murdered by a husband or partner in their own home.

- In 1999, 11,000 calls by women were received by the National Network of Refuges and support services.
- According to the 1996 survey of the general population, eighteen per cent of women had suffered violence at the hands of their partner.
- Over half the women surveyed reported that they knew a women who had experienced such violence. (Donohoe and Gaynor 2003:206)

Child abuse

According to the Child Care Act (1991) a child is 'a person under the age of 18 years other than a person who is or has been married' (cited in Richardson 1999:170). Abuse of children can take different forms. It can be physical, emotional, neglect or sexual. Sexual abuse in Ireland has only been highlighted since around the 1980s, but as with domestic violence, the full extent is not known. Statistics provided by the Department of Health and Children show that in 1995 there were 6,415 reports of alleged child abuse, about a third of which were confirmed cases. 'Child abuse statistics show that the number of cases that have been reported to the health boards have more than doubled between 1992 and 1999' (Donohoe and Gaynor 2003:213).

THE FAMILY AND SOCIAL CARE: LEGISLATION AND SERVICES (VOLUNTARY AND STATUTORY) PROTECTING FAMILIES AND CHILDREN

1. The Domestic Violence Act 1996
2. The 1987 Status of Children Act
3. The 1988 Adoption Act
4. The 1991 Childcare Act

The above list mentions some of the legislation that gives the state the right to intervene and to take action to protect children and families. Agencies involved in meeting their needs should problems such as domestic violence arise include:

- The Department of Justice, Equality and Law Reform/Gardaí
- The Department of the Environment and Local Government
- The Department of Social and Family Affairs
- The Department of Health and Children

Other agencies working in the area of child support and protection are the Barnardos Child and Family Services and the ISPCC.

According to Donohoe and Gaynor, 'in Ireland, family accommodation in refuges has risen marginally from 90 rooms in 1998 to 93 in 2002 in 17 refuges countrywide . . . To adequately meet the need, one refuge per 10,000 population is recommended (that would mean 300–400 refuge places in Ireland' (2003:207).

The family is an important social institution which helps hold society together. Sociologists' interest in the area lies in its role as a site of socialisation, a structuring basis of society, to its importance in influencing policy issues (e.g. patterns of work, childcare, etc.) (www.pshare.com). The family is a complex and dynamic concept and this is evident in the changes that have taken place in the nature and structure of the family in Irish society. According to Tovey and Share, 'in looking to the future we can begin to discern some important changes' (2003:247). Among these changes we can expect to see:

- increasing numbers of people remaining single
- a rise in the number of one-child families
- more gay and lesbian couples
- more voluntarily child-free people.

6

Social Stratification in Irish Society

CHAPTER OBJECTIVES
After reading this chapter you should be able to:
* define social stratification
* describe the systems of stratification
* explain the concept of social class
* describe class structure in Irish society in relation to health, housing, consumption patterns and education
* describe social mobility in Irish society.

SOCIAL STRATIFICATION DEFINED

'Social stratification: The division of a society into a number of strata, hierarchically arranged groupings' (Mann 1983:366).

Social stratification is the term used by sociologists to describe the inequalities that exist between individuals and groups within human societies (Giddens 2001:282). While people may think of stratification in terms of assets or property, it also refers to all forms of inequality based on class, gender, ethnicity, age, religious affiliation, etc. People are ranked hierarchically according to their possession of these attributes. 'This sort of ranking leads to groups of people being classified into layers or strata – like geological rock formations – hence the term stratification' (Marsh 2000:268). Societies can be seen as consisting of 'strata' in a hierarchy, with the more favoured at the top and the less privileged nearer the bottom.

Virtually all societies have some form of stratification or structured inequalities that are organised and that persist over time. In nearly 'all societies some people are regarded as more important than others, more worthy of respect or more useful than others either within the society as a whole or in certain categories' (O'Donnell 2002:119). According to Babbie

(1988:124) large segments of society are stratified, for example men generally do better than women, whites do better than blacks, younger people do better than older people. Different societies value these characteristics differently but it is based on them that individuals and groups enjoy equal (or unequal) access to rewards. Modernisation of society has created new patterns of social inequality that needed to be understood. 'The analysis of social and economic inequality was a central concern of sociology from its inception' (Bilton *et al.* 2002:72). According to sociologists, social stratification is a matter of four basic principles.

Principles of stratification

1. Social stratification is a characteristic of society, not a reflection of individual differences.
2. Social stratification persists over generations.
3. Social stratification is universal but variable.
4. Social stratification involves not just inequality but beliefs (Macionis and Plummer 2002:178).

SYSTEMS OF STRATIFICATION

Most societies have some form of general stratification placing certain groups of people in superior and inferior positions, a hierarchy of prestige and power. Historically four basic systems of stratification have existed in society. These are slavery, caste, estate and class.

Slavery

This is the oldest and most extreme form of stratification or inequality in which some individuals are literally owned by others as property. 'Between the fifteenth and the nineteenth centuries the industrial and financial might of modern European powers was directly related to the trade in African slaves. This slave labour was crucial to the economic development of the New World and the establishment of black populations in the Americas and the Caribbean' (Marsh 2000:269). Although the forms that slavery has taken have been highly variable, the majority of slaves were deprived of almost all human rights. As a formal institution, slavery has gradually been eradicated but has not yet completely disappeared. According to Macionis and Plummer, although the British Empire abolished slavery in 1833 and the American Civil War brought slavery in the US to an end in 1865, '. . . it [slavery] still persists in a variety of forms in many parts of the world today'

(2002:181). Bales, an English social scientist, suggests that the system of slavery that exists today is different from traditional slavery. He refers to it as modern slavery which is 'not about direct ownership but about control through violence, usually with major elements of economic exploitation' (Bales 2000, cited in Macionis and Plummer 2002:181). He believes that across the world there are about twenty-seven million people in modern slavery, which include those in:

- forced labour
- debt bondage
- prostitution
- servile marriage.

Usually modern slaves are found amongst the 'poor, the uneducated, the low-status groups of society: frequently, of course, these are women and children' (Ibid.). Slavery is a closed system of stratification and agencies such as Anti-Slavery International continue to monitor the use of forced labour as well as child prostitution on a global scale (Marsh 2000:269).

Caste

This system of stratification is mainly associated with Indian society and the Hindu religion. It is based on a system of religious belief that cannot be changed and is therefore a closed system of stratification. The Hindu belief in reincarnation (rebirth) states that individuals who do not abide by the rituals and duties of their caste will be reborn in an inferior position in their next incarnation. The caste position you occupy is determined at birth, you cannot change it throughout your life. 'Caste systems structure the type of contact that can occur between members of different ranks' (Giddens 2001:282).

In a caste system, birth determines the shape of people's lives in four crucial ways:

1. Traditional caste groups are linked to occupation, so that generations of a family perform the same type of work.
2. Caste systems ensure that people marry others of the same ranking (endogamy).
3. Caste systems guide everyday life so that people remain in the company of 'their own kind'.
4. Caste systems are based on strong cultural and religious beliefs (Macionis and Plummer 2002:182).

This system was officially abolished in 1947, but still survives in rural areas as do the beliefs on which it was based (3,000 years) (Marsh 2000:270). The following outline of the Hindu caste system described by O'Donnell provides an overview of how 'the structure of society is divinely ordained and individuals are obliged to accept it and to carry out their duties with it, without ambition to change (dharma)' (Marsh 2000:270).

THE HINDU CASTE SYSTEM

BRAHMANS (e.g. priests and teachers)
▼
KSHATRIYAS (e.g. warriors, landlords)
▼
VAISHYAS (e.g. merchants, traders)
▼
SUDRAS (e.g. peasants, servants)
▼
HARYANS (untouchables)
▼
SOCIAL OUTCASTS (e.g. leathermakers, sweepers)

- Each caste subdivided into thousands of Jatis (subcastes) with their own restrictions and rituals.
- No mobility between castes was possible.
- Kharma (Hindu belief in reincarnation) results in those who rigidly obey the caste's code (Dharma) being reborn into a higher caste. Those who do not obey the code are reborn into a lower caste.
- Outcastes are segregated – they would pollute higher castes.
- Although higher castes are often richer than lower, this is not necessarily so. The purest 'Brahmans' may reject all possessions, a haryan leathermaker may become rich. (Adapted from O'Donnell 2002:123)
- The Brahmans, Kshatriyas, Vaishyas and Sudras are the four main groups Hindus can belong to.
- The 1901 census identified 2,378 main castes and 1,700 subcastes within just one of these main castes. (*Ibid.*:123)
- Caste systems existed in other societies, such as in the former apartheid system of South Africa where black and white were segregated and stratified. South Africa banned marriage and even sex between the races until 1985 (Macionis and Plummer 2002:182).

Estates

Medieval Europe was a feudal system based on the idea of estates. The feudal estates consisted of different strata or layers. Three major groups were identified:

1. the nobility or aristocracy
2. the clergy
3. the commoners.

Each of these groups had differing obligations and rights towards each other. This system was closely related to property and political power with land ownership as the key. Although it was not encouraged, movement between the strata was tolerated, especially in towns. It did allow some degree of social mobility. (Marsh 2000:270)

Class

'A class can be defined as a large-scale grouping of people who share common economic resources, which strongly influence the type of lifestyle they are able to lead' (Giddens 2001:282).

The social class system is a system of stratification that results from the unequal distribution of wealth, power and prestige. It is considered an open system of stratification as unlike the other systems it claims to be based on individual achievement. For example, a person who works hard or studies hard can change their social class position. According to Marsh, 'Class position is largely determined by an individual's place within the economic system and is to some extent achieved' (2000:270).

THE CONCEPT OF SOCIAL CLASS

'Sociologists argue that class position is a major determinant of life conditions and resources, including access to property and income, to education, to housing, to good health and to power' (Drudy 1995:295). Class systems are considered to be the main form of social stratification in western industrialised societies today, and because of this the concept of class is central in social theory and analysis.

The economic system of capitalism resulted in the emergence of social classes. Capitalism, according to O'Donnell, is an economic system in 'which some people are free to sell what is produced for their own profit, while others are legally free to sell their labour where they like' (2002:124). The following highlights the main characteristics of class which makes it different to the other systems of stratification:

1. According to Giddens, 'Classes are not established by legal or religious provisions, membership is not based on inherited position as specified either legally or by custom' (2001:282).

2. A person's class position is in some part achieved, not ascribed or given at birth as in some other systems of stratification. With this system 'merit' is rewarded and enables a person to rise to a higher social stratum. Movement (or mobility) upwards and downwards in the class structure is possible. A class system is more open so that people who gain schooling and skills may experience some social mobility in relation to their parents and siblings. The fluidity of this system blurs class distinctions making them difficult to define. 'Social boundaries also break down as people immigrate from abroad or move from the countryside to the city, lured by greater opportunity for education and better jobs' (Lipset and Bendix 1967, cited in Macionis and Plummer 2002:184). Class systems put no formal restrictions on inter-marriage between people from different classes.

3. Classes depend on economic differences between groups of individuals – inequalities in the possession and control of material resources. According to O'Donnell, 'As feudalism died out and social "classes" became established those families which occupied high-prestige positions under the old order often continued to do so, as they had the wealth or "capital" available to invest in developing their lands, industry or commerce in order to produce a surplus income or "profit"' (2002:124).

4. Class systems operate mainly through large-scale connections of an impersonal kind. For example, inequalities of pay and working conditions are one major base of class differences. Giddens states that 'these affect all the people in specific occupational categories, as a result of economic circumstances prevailing in the economy as a whole' (2001:283). However, it is important to remember that the class we are born into (class of origin) has a huge influence on how we live our lives and on where we end up (class of destination) (Donohoe and Gaynor 2003:71).

CLASS STRUCTURE IN IRISH SOCIETY

'Irish society is often thought of as a classless society' (Tovey and Share 2003:160). Such a statement may suggest that class boundaries are not as severe or defined in Ireland and as a result may seem less constraining, but 'the reality is that they are more rigid and harder to penetrate than in many other societies' (*Ibid.*:161). Social class is the main form of social stratification in Ireland and in western industrialised societies today. Researchers studying the area have focused on how race, gender, etc., have influenced socio-economic status, but classification by occupation tends to be most common. 'Officially in Ireland a person's social class is measured according to occupation. The social class of children is derived from the occupation of their parent(s)' (Donohoe and Gaynor 2003:71). According to Donohoe and Gaynor there are huge inequalities between the classes in the distribution of wealth and income. It is estimated that ten per cent of the population own nearly half of the wealth in the country, therefore ninety per cent of the population share the other half, but not equally (*Ibid.*:71).

Ireland's late and sudden industrialisation brought with it huge changes to the class structure. The pre-industrial class structure was transformed and new lines of class distinction began to emerge. 'However, it was not until the 1960s and 1970s that any major transformation in the economy or in the social structure occurred' (IPA 1992:98). Rottman and Hanna attempted to trace the implications of changes in employment in class terms during the course of industrialisation in Ireland during that period. They distinguished four main class groupings based on the types and levels of resources which families possess:

1. A 'bourgeoisie' made up of substantial property owners (in both the agricultural and non-agricultural sectors) who employ hired labour.
2. A 'petit bourgeoisie' consisting of four categories of farmers and one of non-farmers who are self-employed and do not employ labour.
3. A middle class comprised of non-manual employees, divided by educational qualifications into higher professionals, lower professionals and intermediate non-manual employees.
4. A working class which is divided into four different categories: skilled manual, service, semi-skilled and unskilled manual workers (cited in IPA 1992:99).

Their findings related to male employment as up until the 1981 census of population women had their social class ascribed to them according to the occupation of their father or husband.

'Now a woman's social class is derived from her own occupation but some difficulties remain, for example in relation to the classification of the role of mother/housewife/homemaker' (Donohoe and Gaynor 2003:71). According to findings presented by the IPA, the class structure of Irish society was characterised by the following:

1920s/1930s
- More than half of the population was engaged in agriculture. Irish society was predominantly 'petit bourgeoisie'.

1940s/1950s
- Decline in numbers of agricultural labourers.
- Decline in number and proportion of farmers who were employers.
- Increase in numbers employed in non-agricultural sectors.
- High levels of emigration as there were not enough jobs in non-agricultural sectors to absorb those leaving agriculture.

1960s
Industrialisation resulted in:
- Growth in number of higher professionals.
- Increase in numbers of skilled manual workers.
- Decline in number of small shop-keepers.
- Marginalisation of the unskilled manual worker.

1970s
Shape of modern class structure became apparent.
- Dominant categories of large employers, higher professionals and skilled manual workers.
- Seventy per cent of those at work were salary and wage earners compared to forty-eight per cent in 1926.
- In 1979, twenty per cent of the workforce were professionals, administrators and senior salaried employees.
- Numbers of unskilled and semi-skilled workers declined by nearly half in the period between 1951 and 1979. (IPA 1992:101)

Class and health

'Research on varying aspects of health internationally indicates the powerful effects of socio-economic differentials and data specific to the Irish situation although not extensive, is convincing and consistent with international findings' (Collins and Shelley 1997, cited in Quin 1999:40). Findings show that poorer people, on average, live shorter lives and are subject to more ill-health at an earlier age than their rich counterparts, which leads to what Nolan describes as 'a double injustice – life is short where quality is poor!' (1989, cited in Quin 1999:41). Unemployment also is strongly related to poorer-than-average health.

Table 6:1 Socio-economic Group Related to Standardised Mortality Rates

Socio-economic group	15–24	25–34	35–44	45–54	55–64
	(Death rate per 1,000)				
Farmers	0.9	0.8	1.4	5.6	14.8
Higher professional	0.2	0.3	0.8	3.5	12.8
Salaried employees	1.0	0.6	1.5	3.6	15.2
Skilled manual	0.9	0.7	1.9	6.2	18.7
Unskilled manual	1.9	1.5	3.4	10.7	31.6

(Source: Cleary and Tracy 1997, cited in Tovey and Share 2003:285)

The above table provides evidence of strong links between health status and socio-economic differentials.

Housing

In Ireland housing type and residential patterns clearly relate to social class differences. According to figures presented by the IPA (1992:117):

* In 1973 seventy-six per cent of households with professional or managerial heads were owner occupiers (either owned outright or mortgaged), compared with forty-nine per cent of skilled manual households and thirty-three per cent of semi-skilled and unskilled manual households.
* In 1991 there were 1,006,506 permanent housing units in the state. (CSO 1991, cited in Silke 1999:51)

Quality of accommodation is a central issue in housing policy and is often measured in terms of household facilities, such as running water, flush toilet, age of dwelling and over-crowding. A survey of the housing stock was undertaken in 1990. 'The national survey which involved a survey of over 20,000 housing units, found 5.5 per cent of housing units were unfit for habitation' (Finn 1992, cited in Silke 1999:53).

Consumption patterns

There is a relationship between consumption and social class. Research by the Combat Poverty Agency in 1992 (cited in Tovey and Share 2003:490) compared the weekly spending patterns of two household types, one with an income (described as an average family) and one relying on unemployment payments. The surplus money (that left after paying for food, fuel, housing, transport, etc.) showed differences in consumption. 'The family on unemployment payments spent a higher proportion of its income (but a lower absolute amount) on drink and tobacco than the "average" family, but the "average" family spent a much higher proportion on clothing, shoes and services of various kinds (mainly related to leisure and recreation such as going to the cinema, or out for a meal, getting clothes dry-cleaned or hair cut, caring for a family pet).'

Education

'In spite of considerable progress in recent years the best estimates for 1995 suggest that about 5,000 students each year leave school without any qualification and that a further 8,000 leave before taking the Leaving Certificate' (Clancy 1999:91).

According to Clancy (1999), these differential qualifications of school leavers are directly related to parents' social background. An analysis of three cohorts of school leavers in the early 1990s revealed the following:

- twenty-two per cent of school leavers left without completing the Leaving Cert.
  - forty-seven per cent of these were children of unskilled manual backgrounds
  - three per cent of these were children from higher professional backgrounds (Ibid.:91)
- Over half the children of those in the higher professional social group leave school with five or more Leaving Certificate honours.
  - Only four per cent of those with parents who are unskilled manual workers do the same. (Tovey and Share 2003:216)

For those who attained a Leaving Certificate, the percentage going on to third-level education also varied by socio-economic group and level of attainment in the Leaving Certificate. According to Clancy, after analysing entrants to third-level education for the period 1980–98, 'while participation rates had increased significantly for nearly all occupation or class groups substantial inequalities of access remain'. He found that:

- Fifty-eight per cent of entrants came from just four socio-economic groups: higher professional, lower professional, employers and managers and farmers.

- The other socio-economic groups (non-manual, skilled, semi-skilled, unskilled manual workers, own-account workers and agricultural workers) made up only forty-one per cent of entrants. These groups make up sixty-three per cent of the population. (2001, cited in Tovey and Share 2003:218)

There is a strong link between lack of qualifications and unemployment. The following statistics provided by Tovey and Share provide evidence of this:

- In 1993 seventy-eight per cent of those without a formal qualification remained unemployed after leaving school.
- For those who had a Leaving Certificate this figure dropped to just under thirty per cent.
- In 1997 sixty-three per cent of those unemployed had not finished secondary education.

'The class into which we are born influences where we live, how we spend our leisure time, the papers we read, our educational prospects and our earning potential' (Donohoe and Gaynor 2003:71).

SOCIAL MOBILITY IN IRELAND

'Social mobility refers to the movement of people between different levels of the class structure from one occupational group to another' (IPA 1992:107). Sociologists are interested in social mobility for the following reasons:

1. It can give an indication of the life chances of members of a society. It can give an indication of how open a society actually is, for example to what degree does a person's background influence their opportunities in later life?
2. The rate of mobility can have important effects on class formation. Giddens suggests 'that if the rate of social mobility is low, class solidarity and class cohesion will be high' (cited in IPA 1992:107).
3. People's attitudes and aspirations can be affected by social mobility. (*Ibid.*)

Mobility within the class structure is usually considered to be upwards or downwards, but it is also:

Intergenerational: this refers to a person's position in the class system in relation to their parents.

Intragenerational: this refers to a person's position in the structure in relation to other positions they have had at different stages in their life.

Changes in the occupational structure in Ireland brought changes in mobility patterns. 'In the first half of the twentieth century opportunities open to Irish people depended heavily on whether their family owned property such as a farm or small business. Those set to inherit a position in a family enterprise could stay in Ireland. The rest, generally, had to emigrate or enter the religious life . . .' (Tovey and Share 2003:165).

Movement from an economy based mainly on agriculture meant that many left farming. Industrialisation was not happening at a pace quick enough to absorb those leaving and as a result many were forced to emigrate. 'In 1961 half the gainfully employed men in Ireland worked in farming, this had decreased to a fifth by 1981' (Whelan 1995, cited in Tovey and Share 2003:162). Research carried out by Breen *et al.* (1990), Whelan (1995), Allen (1998), all cited in Tovey and Share (2003:163) provides findings that reflect changes in the class structure and mobility patterns in Irish society. The movement from a society dominated by small family businesses and self-employment to one where individuals are employees in large business has resulted in the following:

- By the mid-1980s nearly three-quarters of males at work were employed in businesses not owned by their family.
- There was an increase in the number of men in the managerial, skilled manual and white collar occupations.
- There was a decline in unskilled and semi-skilled occupations.
- A study conducted in the late 1980s showed that two-fifths of men aged between twenty and sixty-four moved into a class position different to that of their parents.
- Ireland had low levels of upward mobility from the working class to the professional and managerial class.
- Women working outside the home still tend to be found in a restricted range of occupations, primarily professional and managerial.
- Women remain largely excluded from the inheritance of productive property such as agricultural land.
- Women change class through marriage.
- Women are more likely to experience downward mobility. (2003:164/165)

Occupational structure influences and effects mobility patterns but what about those who do not have occupations, who are not in the paid labour force? According to Drudy, 'In Ireland this is the condition of a very large proportion of the adult population' (1995:306).

Table 6:2 Working Males: Changes in Class Categories 1951–90

(Percentages rounded up)	1951 (%)	1961 (%)	1971 (%)	1981 (%)	1990 (%)
Employers and self-employed	38	36	28	19	18
Employees					
• Upper middle class	5	8	11	16	18
• Lower middle class	14	16	18	20	20
• Skilled manual	10	12	17	20	18
• Semi/unskilled					
– agricultural	11	8	5	3	3
– non-agricultural	14	13	14	11	9
Total at work	100	100	100	100	100
Total unemployed	4	6	7	10	16

(Source: Breen and Whelan, cited in Tovey and Share 2003:163)

Drudy refers to the 'underclass' and differentiates them from the working class. The underclass is made up of 'the poor, the long-term unemployed, substance abusers and marginalized groups such as Travellers' (Tovey and Share 2003:161). A definition of the underclass given by Whelan (cited in Drudy 1995:311) sees it as a social grouping with three features:
1. prolonged labour market marginality
2. greater deprivation than is general for the manual working class
3. the possession of its own sub-culture.

While opportunities have increased to enable people to move into a better position in society, inequalities do exist. While people are stratified according to attributes such as race, ethnicity, gender, etc. Breen and Whelan conclude with the statement that 'what most determines one's life chances or eventual position in society is not one's gender but the class or occupational position of the family into which one is born' (cited in Tovey and Share 2003:165).

7

Gender Socialisation

CHAPTER OBJECTIVES
After reading this chapter you should be able to:
- define gender
- explain what is meant by gender socialisation
- describe the sexual division of labour – women and the Irish labour market
- describe the relationship between gender and education
- discuss changing gender roles.

GENDER DEFINED

'Gender is the word used to describe social and personality differences between women and men. It refers to that which society defines as masculine and feminine' (Webb and Tossell 1999:47).

Sex refers to the biological differences between male and female. Gender, on the other hand, refers to the socially constructed and variable categories of masculine and feminine. Bilton *et al.* describe 'gender as the cultural gloss put on a natural foundation of sex' (2002:131). When we meet someone for the first time, we notice whether they are male or female. Such information enables us to interact with them in a socially acceptable manner. Clarke *et al.* (2000:154) argue that children pick up the appropriate sex role by imitating the same-sex parent and being reinforced for behaving in a manner that the particular culture expects of a boy or a girl. 'By reinforcing masculine behaviour in a boy, either parent could ensure that he showed masculine behaviour, similarly for feminine behaviour in a girl' (*Ibid.*:154). Children learn to behave as 'boy' or 'girl' and also learn that they should not cross the gender roles if possible.

The concept of gender changes over time, and is defined differently between societies and within the same society. We all 'do gender' in our daily social interactions with other people. According to Giddens, 'From tone of voice to gestures and movements to norms of behaviour, all aspects of our existence are gendered. We socially reproduce – make and remake – gender in a thousand minor actions in the course of the day' (2001:106).

GENDER SOCIALISATION

'Socialisation theory offers a straightforward account of the acquisition of gendered identities. Infants are seen as blank slates, waiting to be written on by their environment' (Bilton *et al.* 2002:136).

From the day we are born, the process of gender socialisation begins and infants learn what sex they are and what is expected of them as little boys and girls in their society. Agents of socialisation such as the family, media, education, etc., contribute to the child's understanding of his or her social role. Through constant interactions with people close to them and exposure to the values of their society, 'children gradually internalise the social norms and expectations which are seen to correspond with their sex' (Giddens 2001:108).

There is a lot of research and theorising on gender development, but three broad traditions can be distinguished. These are:

1. **Social learning theories:** These theories suggest that differences in gender behaviour are learned in the same way as all behaviours, through a mixture of rewards, reinforcements and punishments (Macionis and Plummer 2002:298). 'Gender processing begins from the moment of birth when baby girls are traditionally covered in pink blankets and boys in pale blue ones' (Webb and Tossell 1999:48). Boys and girls learn 'sex roles' and 'masculinity or femininity' and are guided to do so by the use of positive and negative sanctions, which reward or restrain behaviour. Boys who receive praise such as 'What a brave boy you are!' or a negative sanction such as 'Boys don't play with dolls' begin to learn and conform to their expected sex role. Children also model or imitate the behaviour of parents, teachers of the same sex and this process also helps children internalise the gender prescriptions of their society. 'If an individual develops gender practices which do not correspond with his or her biological sex – that is, they are deviant – the explanation is seen to reside in inadequate or irregular socialisation' (Giddens 2001:108).

Parents (consciously or unconsciously) tend to treat girls and boys differently in ways that influence their development. For example:

(i)   According to McDonald and Parke (1986), 'parents are far more likely to engage their infant sons in rough physical play – tossing them up in the air or wrestling with them – than they are their daughters' (cited in Bilton *et al.* 2002:136). They argue that the long-term results of that may be the development of physical confidence or aggressiveness in boys.

(ii) Webb and Tossell refer to studies which suggest that mothers have a tendency to breastfeed boys for longer periods than girls. 'This action, whether it is done unconsciously or not, tends to reflect an inclination to foster independence and responsibility on girls (who are later to be the principal caregivers) whilst tolerating dependency in boys' (1999:48).

2. Cognitive theory: This theory suggests that differences in gender emerge through a categorisation process, for example boys place themselves in a 'masculine' category and then organise their experiences around it. (Macionis and Plummer 2002:299)

3. Psychodynamic theories: These are derived from Freud and suggest that 'differences in gender emerge out of emotional struggles between the infant and its caretakers in the earliest years of life' (Macionis and Plummer 2002:299). One of the most influential theories of gender identity is the perspective developed by Nancy Chodorow in her 1978 book *The Reproduction of Mothering*. This theory takes account of the unconscious processes that contribute to a child's learning to feel male or female. For Chodorow this derives from the infant's attachment to its parents from an early age. Her theory places much importance on the mother rather than the father. For her 'masculinity and femininity are rooted in strong emotional structures established very early in life and are very hard to transform' (Macionis and Plummer 2002:299). To understand these emotional structures we have to look at the strong attachments between a child and its mother, in which both the baby boy and baby girl are hugely dependent on the mother. In their early years mothers generally care for infants, while fathers tend to remain more emotionally distant. At some point in time, this attachment has to be broken in order to achieve a separate sense of self. The child is required to become less dependent on the carer, to test its competence against the outside world. This process of breaking away operates differently for girls and boys. The little girl remains attached while the little boy breaks away. Chodorow believes that as a result:

- Girls remain closer to the mother; the little girl does not outgrow her dependency, she maintains a continuous sense of relationship with the mother.
- Boys' experience is different. Their separation is sharper and involves 'repressing the feminine aspects of themselves and rejecting much of the tenderness that was central to that early relationship' (Bilton *et al.* 2002:137).

As a result of these processes, men are likely to:
(i)   be more independent and more competitive when dealing with others
(ii) have difficulty in expressing emotions
(iii) have a more autonomous sense of self. (Macionis and Plummer 2002:299)

According to Giddens, boys 'learn not to be "sissies" or "mummy's boys". As a result, boys are relatively unskilled in relating closely to others, they develop more analytical ways of looking at the world. They take a more active view of their lives, emphasising achievement, but they have repressed their ability to understand their own feelings and those of others' (2001:111).

Girls are more likely to:
(i)   identify with the needs of others more than boys; this asserts itself as a need for mothering later in life
(ii) have more need and greater ability to sustain relationships with others
(iii) have greater empathy with others.

'Chodorow's ideas teach us a good deal about the nature of femininity, and they help us to understand the origins of what has been called male inexpressiveness – the difficulty men have in revealing their feelings to others' (Giddens 2001:111).

This theory has often been criticised by feminists 'who accuse the theory of blaming mothers for reproduction of male power in their sons' (Macionis and Plummer 2002:299).

There is much in the socialisation of men that discourages them from expressing their feelings. From an early age men are pressurised to hide their true feelings, to always appear strong and in control. 'Big boys don't cry' is a clear message throughout childhood which is reinforced in books and other forms of popular culture' (Webb and Tossell 1999:50).

SEXUAL DIVISION OF LABOUR – WOMEN AND THE IRISH LABOUR MARKET

The differences between women's and men's productive work in Ireland are as follows:

1. Far more women than men spend time on housework and caring.
2. More men than women are employed full-time.
3. Men and women who are employed are segregated into very different kinds of occupations.
4. Employed men earn much more than employed women. (Lynch and Morgan 1995:266)

'The world of work remains a key site for the expression of gender difference and the positions that men and women hold in the labour market are a major determinant of wealth, income, power and status' (Tovey and Share 2003:247). Changes in the last decades of the twentieth century had a significant impact on the relationship of Irish women towards the labour market. The following statistics and findings reflect the position of Irish women in the labour market before the economic change that occurred in Ireland:

• In 1926, sixty per cent of women who were employed worked either in agriculture or in domestic service.
• One in ten worked in industry.
• From 1932–73 the 'marriage bar' was in operation. It formally and legally excluded married women from public service. (Tovey and Share 2003:249)

From the 1970s changes in women's position in the labour force began to occur. Expansion in the service industries, from financial to tourism, and investment in Ireland by transnational companies, in no doubt influenced these changes. In this period:

• There was a growth of nine per cent in the number of women employed in the manufacturing industry.
• Women's participation rate in the workforce increased from twenty-eight per cent in 1971 to thirty-nine per cent in 1994.
• By 1994 married women made up half the labour force (Smyth 1997, cited in Tovey and Share 2003:250).
• In 1996 married women in the workforce outnumbered single women. (Galligan 1998, cited in Tovey and Share 2003:250)

The following table, provided by the Central Statistics Office, shows the employment rate for men and women in Ireland from the period 1994 to 2004.

Table 7:1 Ireland: Employment Rate for Men and Women
(percentage of population aged 15–64)

Year	Men	Women
1994	65.9	40.1
1995	67.1	41.6
1996	67.5	43.2
1997	69.1	45.9
1998	71.1	48.1
1999	73.6	51.2
2000	75.7	53.2
2001	76.2	54.0
2002	75.0	55.2
2003	74.7	55.3
2004	75.2	55.8

(Source: adapted from CSO 2004)

According to Donohoe and Gaynor, the majority of women employed in Ireland is concentrated into three job types: clerical, service and technical, and professional. 'Where women are well represented in a workforce they are not proportionately represented in top positions' (1999:121).

Table 7:2 Ireland: Persons in Employment by Occupation, 1999 and 2004

Broad Occupational Group	1999 (000s)		2004 (000s)	
	Men	Women	Men	Women
Craft and related	202.2	16.5	231.3	12.4
Plant and machine operatives	122.1	39.9	130.3	29.1
Managers and administrators	222.0	72.3	227.1	92.1
Sales	49.7	76.9	59.0	93.3
Associate professional and technical	58.1	72.3	72.3	94.8
Professional	83.3	75.2	108.4	103.0
Personal and protective service	67.6	85.1	72.8	112.6
Clerical and secretarial	51.1	148.4	53.1	167.6
Other	92.0	54.6	111.0	66.1
Total	948.0	641.0	1,065.2	771.0

(Source: adapted from CSO 2004)

In 2004 men accounted for fifty-eight per cent of persons in employment. The clerical and secretarial group had the highest proportion of women at 75.9 per cent (CSO 2004).

According to O'Connor, 'Women's hourly earnings across all types of industry are still only four-fifths of men's' (1998, cited in Tovey and Share 2003:253). In 2002 the average income which was liable for payment of social insurance contributions was €26,350 for men and €16,680 for women. Hence, the average income for women was only 63.3 per cent of men's average income (CSO 2004).

'The Human Development Report (1998) states that Irish women are worse off in relation to men and are less likely to be in positions of power than in any other western country' (Donohoe and Gaynor 1999:122).

Table 7:3 Ireland: Average Income Liable for Social Insurance by Age, 2002

Age group	Percentage of age group		Average income (€)		Women's income as percentage of men's
	Men	Women	Men	Women	
Under 25	76.7	76.6	11,151	9,301	83.4
25–34	99.8	89.7	26,349	20,783	78.9
35–44	83.6	66.9	36,267	20,849	57.5
45–54	68.5	55.5	37,709	18,687	49.6
55–64	62.2	39.9	32,641	16,296	49.9
65 and over	46.0	20.7	13,750	9,212	67.0
Total	75.8	61.4	26,350	16,680	63.3

(Source: Dept of Social and Family Affairs, Revenue Commissioners, cited in CSO 2004)

Apart from the obvious benefits of work, that is, to earn money to provide for themselves and their families, work outside the home offers women a source of independence. It also offers them a 'sense of satisfaction, intellectual fulfilment, career progression or a chance to develop personal and social skills (Webb and Tossell 1999:59). Despite this, the rate of Irish women's participation in the workforce remains low by EU standards. According to Galligan, the main barriers to women's equal participation in the labour force include:

• 'the absence of flexible working hours
• the virtual non-existence of childcare facilities
• lack of appropriate training due largely to the negative attitudes of employers' (cited in Tovey and Share 2003:251).

Lynch states that 'the majority (53%) of adult women in the Republic of Ireland are homemakers and therefore mostly unpaid. The comparable proportion of adult men who are homemakers is a meagre 0.5%' (1995:266). Studies such as those by Mahon (1991, cited in Lynch and McLaughlin 1995:250), indicate that women still have primary responsibility for the care of children even when they are in full-time employment. The work a woman does when she arrives home from the office/factory has been referred to as a 'second shift' which involves domestic work, cooking, raising children etc. (Macionis and Plummer 2002:362).

Although the number of women in the workforce is increasing and the range of jobs they do is broadening, 'the demands inherent in the domestic division of labour are continuing to prevent any fundamental change for most women in respect of work. The gendered division of labour still firmly benefits men to the detriment of women' (Bilton *et al.* 2002:313).

GENDER AND EDUCATION

'Gender is central to the experience of education. People's experiences of "being a boy" or "being a girl" are shaped in many ways by the experience of schooling' (Ryan 1997, cited in Tovey and Share 2003:210).

Sociologists are interested in examining how the education process is crucial to the social construction of gender. The educational choices girls make at second level and third level have a huge impact on their educational opportunities. 'At second and third level what is referred to as the "hidden curriculum" is operating, reinforcing traditional male and female roles' (IPA 1992:77).

Dr Damien Hannan carried out a study in 1979 in subject choice in second level schools in Ireland. His results found differences between boys- and girls-only schools in the framing of subjects. The following list presents some of his main findings:

- 'In girls schools, science subjects and mathematical subjects were less likely to form part of the core curriculum.
- At inter cert level, 88 per cent of boys schools require that everyone does science while only 9 per cent of girls schools do.
- In girls schools science was most often offered as a choice against home economics, commerce, art or music.
- Boys schools tended to "stream" more than girls schools' (IPA 1992:81).

Hannan found differences in the school ethos of boys and girls schools. Boys schools had in general a stronger ethos with a clearer career orientation and they offered pupils less choice of subjects' (*Ibid.*:81). Girls schools had a more modest achievement ethos, a liberal curriculum and wider levels of choice for pupils.

More recent research by Lynch (1999) suggests that males and females are now equally represented in many aspects of education, 'with females now making up a slight majority (in the range 51–55%) at post-primary level' (cited in Tovey and Share 2003:210).

He also presented the following findings:

- There is an increased number of women in third-level study.

- Girls out-perform boys in the majority of subjects in the Junior and Leaving Certificates.
- Girls suffer from coeducational schooling, as research has shown that 'girls receive less attention and encouragement from teachers than do boys' (Lynch, cited in Tovey and Share 2003:213).

According to Lynch and Morgan, 'The experiences of women in education in both the Republic and Northern Ireland are fraught with contradictions' (1995:529). They refer to research by Gallagher (1989) and Clancy (1988) which found that in both systems girls:

- get higher aggregate grades than boys in major public examinations
- are more likely to stay in school after the age of sixteen,

but boys:

- outnumber females in third-level education
- outnumber girls in most physical science and technology courses. (Lynch and Morgan 1995:529)

CHANGING GENDER ROLES

'Gender role is a set of socially generated expectations about how men and women should behave' (Clarke *et al.* 2000:127).

Traditionally, the mother stayed at home cooking, looking after the children, while the father went to work. The man would not expect to do domestic tasks such as cleaning, shopping and childcare. His role was an instrumental one, that of economic provider or breadwinner, whilst the woman's role was an expressive one, as nurturer and emotional provider.

According to Macionis and Plummer, 'the traditional view that working for an income is a man's role no longer holds true' (2002:293). Fathers are generally taking a much more active role in homemaking and family care than before, families are spending more time together, more mothers are working (part-time or full-time) to contribute to the household budget. 'Maternal and paternal roles are starting to "converge"' (O'Donnell 2002:201).

Tovey and Share (2003:228) examine three viewpoints about how relationships between men and women have changed in Ireland over the last three decades.

1. The first view is that 'there has been a huge amount of positive change and progress'. This view pays attention to factors that are indicators that Ireland is becoming a 'modern European state'. These factors include:

   - the appointment and prominence of women in politics and high profile occupations, for example President Mary McAleese

- the exposure of abuse against women and children
- the increasing involvement of men in housework and childcare
- the increase in numbers of women in the paid labour force.

2. The second view stresses how little has changed in Ireland. This view refers to the extent of gender inequality that still exists in our society. It refers to discrimination against women in the workplace and to their inferior position in relation to wealth and income. In 1992, 'unpaid work in the household sector was still the principal occupation for over 60 per cent of women' (Fahey 1995:222). According to statistics provided by the Central Statistics Office (2004), 'There was an increasing relative proportion of men in the higher income bands with 10 per cent of men earning €50,000 and over compared to only 2.6 per cent of women.' Failure to address key issues such as childcare, abortion, care of the elderly and other social issues also highlights the widespread inequality that exists between men and women.

3. The last view sees the nature of gender inequality changing. This developing view sees men as increasingly disadvantaged within Irish society. 'There are concerns over the inability of men to adjust to changes in society, education and the workplace and to develop new models of masculinity . . . "boys are the new girls"' (Tovey and Share 2003:299). This viewpoint expresses concern for:

- men's poorer health status and shorter life expectancy
- the academic weakness of boys
- high exposure to violence and higher tendency to suicide
- legal decisions in relation to custody of and access to children.

The essential biological differences between women and men have tended to divide society unequally in terms of women's and men's labour, power roles and expectations. In the past, husband and wife had established roles to play. With the converging of maternal and paternal roles, a new problem may emerge, that of role conflict. For example, both members of a partnership are less certain of what is expected of them. A woman may want a man who is strong and authoritarian to associate with masculinity but at the same time wants someone to make the dinner or change the baby. A man may want a feminine woman who nurtures and cares for the family while at the same time expects her to work to supplement the family income. Both partners may have conflicting wishes. 'Working mothers often experience role conflict and feel guilty that they are neglecting their children . . . Role conflict may be a major source of family conflict' (O'Donnell 2002:52).

Gender roles in Ireland in the first half of the twentieth century were much more distinct than they are today. The existence of different views on the relationships between men and women in Ireland, the new focus on masculinity and the experiences of men, the changing structure of the family and occupational structure in Irish society all show to some extent the complexities of the gender issue.

'It seems we have moved on from a time when women were seen to be naturally weak, emotionally unstable and believed to have smaller brains than men, but belief in a direct biological basis for gender difference and inequality persists' (Tovey and Share 2003:233).

8

Deviance and Social Control

CHAPTER OBJECTIVES:
After reading this chapter you should be able to:
- define deviance and social control
- outline the social foundations of deviance
- explain the theories of crime and deviance
    - positivist theories of individual crime
    - labelling theory (Lemert)
    - theory of differential association (Sutherland)
    - Merton's strain theory
- discuss crime rates in Ireland.

DEVIANCE AND SOCIAL CONTROL DEFINED

'Deviance may be defined as non-conformity to a given set of norms that are accepted by a significant number of people in a community or society' (Giddens 2001:203).

Deviance means any behaviour that differs from the normal. Most simply put, deviance is the breaking of rules – any rules. For Babbie (1988:131) 'it is the violation of established norms' in a society. Deviance is not a simple concept to define and is a much broader concept than crime; 'virtually any act can be defined as deviant. Terry Simmons argues that most people (you and I included) could be labelled deviant by some existing person or groups' (cited in Holdaway 1988:11).

Generally, 'deviance refers to behaviour that is disapproved of and subject to some form of punishment, behaviour that is outside the rules of society and leads to a hostile and critical response from "conventional society"' (Marsh 2000:656).

A person can be considered deviant if:

1. they reject some or all of the norms and values of society, e.g. a hermit
2. they are part of a group whose members accept different beliefs or

practice different behaviour from that common in the general society, e.g. a hippy. (O'Donnell 2002:266)

You can be considered deviant if you speak with your mouth full, stick your tongue out at someone when you meet them for the first time or walk around dressed as a woman when you are in fact a man.

What the above examples show is that you do not have to break the law to be deviant. You can even be called deviant when you try to follow all the rules. Consider the example given by Babbie to illustrate this, 'Spend the day telling everyone the absolute, unvarnished truth and count your remaining friends at the end of the day'! (1988:132).

Some acts are deviant in one society and not another. For example, monogamy is the norm in Irish society, polygamy is not accepted. Homosexuality has been 'decriminalised in many countries but it still carries the death penalty in Iran' (Marsh 2000:657).

'Deviance depends not upon a given action but upon the acceptability of a certain action in a certain circumstance' (O'Donnell 2002:6). Examples of this include:

1. The injection of a drug by a doctor in a hospital may be socially approved, the injection of the same drug by a person 'for kicks' may be condemned and punished.
2. In modern society killing is usually seen as the most serious of offences but when looked at in the context of war, killing can be seen as heroic and people may even be punished for not wanting to take part in killing. (Marsh 2000:657)

Deviant behaviour could be uncommonly good or brave behaviour as well as unacceptable behaviour, such as theft or vandalism. Deviance isn't necessarily bad; it can lead to social change.

Why do most people conform to the rules? According to Marsh this can be answered by referring to two basic types of social control or restraint.

1. **Informal mechanisms of social control** centre around the socialisation process. Children learn from institutions such as the family, education and religion that stealing, cheating etc., are wrong. These informal networks of control range from family and friends through to 'the monitoring done by social workers and psychiatrists, and on to the closed circuit surveillance in shops and shopping centres, the development of electronic tagging and the rise of private policing' (Macionis and Plummer 2002:413).

2. **Formal mechanisms of control** involve legal and formally established sanctions, such as the law, the police and punishment system. The criminal justice system is a society's formal response to crime (Marsh 2000:659). 'A

sanction is a method of enforcing obedience' (O'Donnell 2002:262). These can also be referred to as rewards or punishments to ensure people accept the approved behaviour of their society. Rewards and punishments can be both formal and informal.

Formal rewards can be in the form of a bonus or promotion at work for employees who have worked hard in the socially approved ways to achieve their benefits or success. An informal way of rewarding a person would include a child's 'being given sweets for helping out his/her mam'. A formal negative sanction or punishment would include a prison sentence for a child abuser while an informal sanction would include ignoring someone who has offended us. 'Positive sanctions tend to be more effective than negative ones in ensuring social control' (O'Donnell 2002:264).

Social control aims to ensure that people abide by the general rules and expectations of the society in which they live. 'Sociologists studying deviant behaviour seek to understand why certain behaviours are widely regarded as deviant and how these notions of deviance are applied differentially to people within society' (Giddens 2001:204). It requires that we step back and take a look before we condemn people and their behaviour just because they don't fit well with the norms. After all we should ask whose rules are they anyway. 'The study of deviance, directs our attention to social power, as well as to the influence of social class – the divisions between rich and poor. As we shall see, social norms are strongly influenced by divisions of power and class' (Giddens 2001:204).

THE SOCIAL FOUNDATIONS OF DEVIANCE

Deviance, as well as conformity, is shaped by society. According to Macionis and Plummer (2002:418) there are three social foundations of deviance:

1. Deviance varies according to cultural norms – behaviour is only considered deviant when examined in relation to cultural norms. The norms that govern Irish life differ to those that govern the life of someone living in India. Laws also differ from place to place. In some Arab countries a man is permitted to have up to four wives. A man in Irish society who tried to do the same would face prison. In Amsterdam the use of soft drugs is permitted and 'there are even shops for their sale. In the rest of Europe, marijuana is outlawed' (Macionis and Plummer 2002:418).

2. People become deviant as others define them that way – 'Deviance is not a simple quality, present in some kinds of behaviour and absent in others. Rather, it is the product of a process which involves responses of

other people to the behaviour . . .' (Keating, cited in Marsh 2002:209). For example, if you help yourself to stationery in a shop you are stealing and deviant, but if you do so at work by 'borrowing' their supplies, you may not be seen as deviant. Whether such an activity is seen as criminal or not depends on how others perceive, define and respond to the situation. 'Deviance is the result of interaction between rule-breaker and witness and not merely the result of what the rule-breaker does' (Tovey and Share 2000:271).

3. Both rule-making and rule-breaking involve social power – norms and their application are linked to social power. 'The law, Karl Marx asserted, amounts to little more than a strategy by which powerful people protect their interests' (Macionis and Plummer 2002:418).

THEORIES OF CRIME AND DEVIANCE

Positivist theories of individual crime

'Positivist theories focus on the characteristics and causes of a criminal type' (Macionis and Plummer 2002:419).

Much of the early work on crime attempted to explain it as something done by criminals that was essentially biological in character. Sociologists at that time studied groups of convicted criminals and focused on innate qualities within individuals as the source of crime and deviance. They believed that criminal types could be identified by certain anatomical features. An Italian physician, Caesare Lombroso, worked in prisons, and in 1876 declared that criminals have a distinctive physique. 'He investigated the appearance and physical characteristics of criminals, such as the shape of the skull and forehead, jaw size and arm length, and concluded that they displayed traits held over from earlier stages of human evolution' (Giddens 2001:205). He declared that features common to criminals included low foreheads, prominent jaws and cheekbones, protruding ears, excessive hairiness and unusually long arms.

His work was flawed, 'had he looked beyond prison walls, he would have realised that the physical features attributed exclusively to prisoners actually were found throughout the entire population' (Macionis and Plummer 2002:419). Although Lombroso's work was discredited, similar theories emerged. Sheldon in 1949 distinguished three main types of human physique and claimed that one type was directly associated with delinquency. The mesomorph (the muscular, active type), according to the theory, are 'more aggressive and physical and therefore more likely to become delinquent than those of thin physique (ectomorphs) or more fleshy people (encomorphs)' (Giddens 2001:205).

Other researchers looked for psychological explanations of crime. They focused on personality types and looked for psychological defects: 'people who took illegal drugs were (and indeed still commonly are) thought to suffer from personality defects of various sorts, such as a poorly developed super-ego, or excessive narcissism, or were people with "addictive personalities"' (Tovey and Share 2003:310).

The positivist theories (biological or psychological explanations) have three major characteristics. According to David Matza (1964):

1. they focus on the criminal as a specific type of person
2. they look for ways in which criminals differ from others, and
3. they seek out explanations for criminal conduct as in some way of control of the criminal who perpetrates criminal acts (cited in Macionis and Plummer 2002:420).

The main weakness of this approach is that it offers no insight into how some kinds of behaviour come to be defined as deviant in the first place. 'Both biological and psychological approaches to criminality presume that deviance is a sign of something wrong with the individual, rather than with society' (Giddens 2001:207).

Labelling theory

'This theory focuses on the processes by which some people label other members of society as deviant. According to labelling theorists, people's labels rather than actions are important' (Clarke et al. 2000:134).

Labelling theory is the name for the sociological view that people often take on the statuses assigned to them by the opinions of those around them. For example, someone widely and unjustly regarded as a thief may begin stealing. 'A woman, labelled unfairly as sexually loose, may eventually loosen up her sexuality to match this image' (Babbie 1988:39). Labelling is a process by which:

1. people are identified in a particular way
2. they then receive special attention as a result of the label being attached to them
3. they come to be regarded by others and to see themselves in the way they are described by the label. (O'Donnell 2002:266)

Labelling not only affects how others see an individual but also influences the individual's sense of self. Edwin Lemert (1972) made a distinction between primary and secondary deviance. Primary deviance refers to what Lemert called the 'initial act of transgression'; the deviant act remains 'marginal' to the person's self identity – 'a process occurs by which the deviant act is normalised' (Giddens 2001:210).

In some cases, however, normalisation does not occur and the person is labelled as a criminal or delinquent. 'Lemert used the term secondary deviance to describe cases where individuals came to accept the label and see themselves as deviant' (Giddens 2001:210). If this happens, the label can become central to the person's identity and lead to a continuation or intensification of the deviant behaviour. 'The development of secondary deviance is one application of the Thomas theorem which states situations defined as real become real in their consequences' (Macionis and Plummer 1997:213).

Who labels? Labelling theorists stress the importance of power in both the enforcement and the construction of laws. Those with power benefit from it, and those without power are disadvantaged when laws are constructed and enforced. 'Law enforcement by the police and courts is a selective process in which certain social groups are more vulnerable to arrest, prosecution and punishment' (Bilton *et al.* 2002:390). The actions of those doing the labelling are of as much concern as those of the labelled. 'The focus on the process of labelling raises the issue of who has the power to define and impose their definitions of right and wrong on others' (Marsh 2000:663).

According to Giddens, 'By and large, the rules in terms of which deviance is defined are framed by the wealthy for the poor, by men for women, by older people for younger people, and by ethnic majorities for minority groups' (2001:209).

Labelling theory is considered an important approach to studying criminality. It is important because it sees no act as being intrinsically criminal. Acts are seen as being defined as criminal by the powerful, through the formation of laws and their interpretation and enforcement by the guards, courts, etc.

It is along these lines that the theory has also been criticised. For example:

1. There are certain acts such as murder, theft, etc., that are prohibited across nearly all cultures.
2. Labelling theorists neglect the processes that lead to acts defined as deviant.
3. It is not clear whether labelling actually does have the effect of increasing deviant conduct. (Giddens 2001:211)

Theory of differential association: Sutherland

This theory was first described by Edwin Sutherland in 1934. Sutherland advanced that deviance is learned through interaction with others. 'Any person's tendency towards conformity or deviance depends on the relative frequency of association with others who encourage conventional behaviour or norm violation' (Macionis and Plummer 2002:422). He believed that criminal behaviour is learned in interaction with other persons, especially within intimate personal groups, in a process of communication. According to Mann, learning includes:

- techniques of committing the crime and
- the specific direction of motives, drives, attitudes and definitions of legal codes. (1983:93)

Sutherland linked crime with differential association. Most simply put, his idea was that 'in a society that contains a variety of subcultures, some social environments tend to encourage illegal activities whereas others do not. Individuals become delinquent through associating with people who are the carriers of criminal norms' (Giddens 2001:209). For him, criminal activities are learned in much the same way as law-abiding ones. This theory sees criminal behaviour as an expression of general needs and values just as non-criminal behaviour is an expression of the same needs and values. This theory rejects the idea that psychological differences separate criminals from non-criminals.

Merton's strain theory

Robert Merton argues that deviance is generated by the structure and culture of the environment in which the individual lives. For him all societies establish goals of success and provide a means for achieving them. However, there are situations in which people cannot achieve the goals by normal means. Merton uses the term 'anomie' when he refers to these situations (IPA 1992:161). He carried out his study in the US in the 1930s and from its findings found that people in society are oriented to the goals associated with monetary success. For him society placed demands on individuals to accumulate wealth and achieve success, but largely denied them the opportunities to do so effectively. Society wanted people to achieve these goals by approved means; this was the path to conformity. When the institutional means of attaining these goals was denied to an individual they might respond to the situation by deviating in one of four different ways:

- Innovation

- Ritualism
- Retreatism
- Rebellion.

1. Conforming: People who conform are those who accept the goals of their society and set about achieving these goals in a generally acceptable way. The majority of the population falls into this category, i.e. someone who gains wealth and status by hard work and talent.

2. Innovation: The innovators are people who accept the goals of the society but not the accepted means of achieving them, e.g. a person who seeks wealth but who does so by means of robbery, gambling, etc. For some innovators, opportunities to achieve wealth by any other means are not available to them.

3. Ritualism: Ritualists are people who do not believe in the goals, but go through the socially approved motions for fear of disapproval. 'For example, a couple may reject the values of society in relation to marriage, but still do marry, even though they do not regard it as sinful to live together without marriage' (O'Donnell 2002:259).

4. Retreatism: Retreatists avoid decisions on, or reject, society's goals or methods of achieving them and withdraw from society as much as possible. This group could include some alcoholics, drug addicts, hermits, etc.

5. Rebellion: Rebels openly reject the values of society, both the goals and the means of achieving them. They usually advocate radical alternatives to the existing social order.

Table 8:1 Merton's Theory of Anomie and its Adaptations

	Cultural goals, e.g. wealth, success	Institutionalised means, e.g. college, hard work, etc.
1. Conformity	+	+
2. Innovation	+	−
3. Ritualism	−	+
4. Retreatism	−	−
5. Rebellion	+−	+−

(+) = signifies acceptance
(−) = signifies rejection
(+−) = signifies rejection and substitution of new goals and standards

(Source: adapted from Holdaway 1988:72)

'According to Merton, the "strain" between a culture's emphasis on wealth and the limited opportunity to get rich gives rise, especially among the poor, to theft, the selling of illegal drugs, etc.' (Macionis and Plummer 2002:420).

According to Tovey and Share, this theory 'assumes that people are not naturally aggressive and selfish but that these qualities are fostered in them by an anomic society – one which encourages people to believe that only wealth and consumption can give their lives meaning and worth but which nonetheless denies many of them the chance to achieve these goals' (2003:305).

This approach explains crime in terms of the structure and culture of society rather than in terms of the individual. However it has been criticised for offering explanations of crime that are too generalised, for example not all people who have restricted opportunities turn to crime (Marsh 2000:663).

CRIME RATES IN IRELAND

'Crime may be defined as an act that breaks the criminal law, it can be followed by criminal proceedings and formal punishment' (Marsh 2000:656).

According to McCullagh (1999:410) 'one of the major changes in Irish society over the past 30 years has been the growth in the level of recorded crime and in the accompanying perception that there is now a significant crime problem in that society'. The rise has been attributed to increasing levels of violent crime, such as murder and assault, and of property crimes such as burglary and car theft, many of which are felt to be drug related (*Ibid.*). 'While there has been concern in relation to the rise in the homicide rate, the official statistics suggest that violent crime is at a very low level in Ireland' (O'Connell 2002, cited in Tovey and Share 2003:300). The statistics provided by the 2003 Annual Report on crime reported that 'there were 45 murders recorded in 2003 which was a decrease of seven over that recorded in 2002. When murders and manslaughters are combined, the total of 52 recorded in 2003 represents a decrease of 12 per cent of the 59 recorded in the previous year.' According to O'Mahony, 'the statistics indicate that the level of violent crime is about half the US rate, a third of the EU average and a quarter of that for Denmark or England and Wales' (2002, cited in Tovey and Share 2003:300).

Sexual assaults against adults and children are now recognised as a major social and criminal problem in Ireland. In 1997 there were 279 sex offenders in our prisons, a number comprising twelve per cent of all adult male prisoners in Irish prisons (Murphy 1998, cited in Cotter 1999:298).

In 1996 there were 14,285 offences committed involving juveniles (An Garda Síochána, 1996). This figure increased to 19,915 in 2003. While the incidence of some offences decreased, such as burglary and vehicle offences, there was a steady increase in the number of detections relating to drink offences. For example drink-related offences accounted for seventeen per cent of referrals in 2001 and for 20.7 per cent in 2003 (An Garda Síochána 2003).

'In recent years around about 600,000 offences per annum have been known to the Gardaí. Over 80 per cent of these (half a million) are non-indictable offences – misdemeanours not thought serious enough to warrant trial by jury, but which can be summarily dealt with by a district court' (Tovey and Share 2003:300). While these crimes are generally not seen as serious they can include offences that have a major impact, such as drink-driving, joyriding and some assaults (O'Mahony 2002, cited in Tovey and Share 2003:300). They also present the following statistics:

1. The majority of offences are traffic offences such as speeding, driving with no tax or insurance.
2. Of approximately 100,000 'indictable offences' recorded annually since the early 1980s over ninety-five per cent have been property crimes.
3. The figure for indictable crimes, which peaked in 1999, was just over 81,000.

According to O'Mahony (2000:3), Ireland has seen an emergence in:

• violent and intimidatory crimes like gangland assassination, torture and murder of isolated old people for their money
• a growth in more vicious crime
• an exposure of previously hidden crime such as child sex abuse, rape and 'white collar crime', at all levels in society
• a growth in serious levels of drug abuse which has impacted on the nature of crime – from individual addicts to organised criminal gangs.

Although official statistics rarely provide full information on the background of offenders, such information that is available tends to suggest that the majority of crimes are committed by young adult working-class males (IPA 1992:170). According to research carried out by Paul O'Mahony on prisoners in Mountjoy Prison, the 'typical prisoner was male, had left school before the legal minimum age, had limited experience of the world of work and was likely to have serious emotional and personal problems, such as a history of drug abuse or psychiatric difficulties' (cited in

McCullagh 1999:410). Research by Rottman (1984) provides an analysis of people 'apprehended' for indictable offences in the Dublin Metropolitan Area. He found that:

- most of these people were male (eighty-four per cent)
- were very young (one-quarter were under sixteen and a further half between seventeen and twenty)
- eighty per cent of the seventeen- to twenty-year-olds were unemployed
- they came from specific locations in Dublin that at the time were socially or physically deprived. (cited in Tovey and Share 2003:305)

According to the IPA (1992:170) women commit far fewer crimes than men, for example the Annual Reports on crime 'show that around 10 to 15 per cent of those convicted of offences in any year are women' (Bacik 2002, cited in Tovey and Share 2003:135).

Who are the victims of crime? A survey carried out by Breen and Rottman in 1985 provided the following findings of the most likely victims:

- those in higher social classes
- young middle-aged
- living in middle-class housing estates. (Cited in Tovey and Share 2003:305)

'In one year in the 80s the increase in serious crime was greater than the total amount of such crime in the one year of 1947' (O'Mahony 1999:120). He referred to Rottman, who he considered was the first person to address the effects of modernisation on crime in Ireland. Rottman's 1980 study suggested that crime rates in Ireland prior to the mid-1960s 'were such as to be almost imperceptible and no signs of pending increases could be found'. His explanation for these low levels of crime included:

1. Ireland's stagnant economy
2. the very high level of emigration
3. a highly conservative political and social culture.

He associated increasing crime rates from the late 1960s on with:

1. intense and rapid modernisation
2. a shift from an agricultural to an industrial economy
3. growth in affluence and Ireland's becoming a more stratified society
4. greater availability of desirable and stealable goods such as cars.

'The new patterns of criminal activity typically associated with industrialisation and urbanisation are an increase in the incidence of property crime, high levels of juvenile delinquency and female crime, and patterns of crime that are more sophisticated' (IPA 1992:173).

Although our crime figures remain low by international standards, the last twenty to thirty years 'have seen a very dramatic decline in the average Irish person's sense of personal security and interpersonal trust' (O'Mahony 2000:3).

As sociologists we need to become aware of the existence and extent of crime in our society. We need to try to identify the possible causes of crime if we hope to reduce or eradicate it.

9

Ageing and Older People

CHAPTER OBJECTIVES

After reading this chapter you should be able to understand:

- growing old – biology and culture (a demographic profile)
- the transitions and problems of ageing
  - retirement
  - social isolation
  - poverty and inequalities
  - abuse of the elderly
  - ageism and discrimination
  - death and dying
  - bereavement

GROWING OLD – BIOLOGY AND CULTURE (A DEMOGRAPHIC PROFILE)

An increasing proportion of the population is made up of elderly members in our society. According to the Central Statistics Office (2002) there are over 436,000 persons over the age of sixty-five years in Ireland. People are living longer and longer. Walker and Maltby (1997, cited in Macionis and Plummer 2002:327) provide the following statistics that reflect this marked increase in life expectancy:

- Within the EU, the average percentage of people over sixty-five rose from 10.6 per cent in 1960 to fourteen per cent in 1991, and was predicted to rise to approximately thirty per cent by 2020. They also found differences across countries: Ireland has the youngest population of EU countries and Sweden has the oldest (followed closely by Germany, France and the UK).
- Italy has the highest proportion of the elderly in the world – in 2000, out of a population of fifty-seven million, nearly ten million were over sixty-five; 17.6 per cent of the population.

- Women outnumber men in the elderly population (due to their greater longevity).
- The discrepancy increases with advancing age: at ages seventy to seventy-four there are roughly four women for every three men, at eighty to eighty-four there are two women for every man, and by ninety-five the ratio becomes three to one (Macionis and Plummer 2002:327).

Table 9:1 Proportions of Over-65s in Selected European Countries, 1993 and Projections for 2025

Country	1993 (%)	2025 (%)
Sweden	18.6	21.2
Italy	15.9	25.1
Britain	15.8	19.0
Germany	15.1	22.9
Greece	14.8	23.9
Poland	10.7	16.4
Turkey	4.4	9.2

(Source: adapted from Giarchi and Abbot 1997, cited in Cole 1999:70)

This ageing of the population is general throughout Europe and may create an economic advantage for those countries with younger populations. 'In Europe, Italy has the greatest proportion of older people (22.7% estimated for 2020), while the Irish Republic has the youngest population (with older people comprising 15.9% of the population by 2020' (O'Donnell 2002:228).

The following information provides the principal demographic results from the 2002 census in Ireland.

Table 9:2 The Elderly Population in Ireland

	Aged 65 years and over	Aged 70 years and over	Aged 75 years and over
Persons	441,684	306,299	192,829
Males	191,590	125,383	73,094
Females	250,094	180,916	119,735

(Source: Census 2002 CSO)

'In France the age of 121 has already been achieved. At the moment women are seven times as likely as men to become centenarians' (Denscombe 1998, cited in Marsh 2000:545).

The following highlights population projections for the elderly population in Ireland:

1. The elderly population is projected to increase by 119,000 persons or 29.5 per cent in the period 1991–2011.
2. There are projected to be 51,000 more persons aged eighty years or more.
3. The number of older persons living alone will rise by more than 41,000 persons.
4. Both the Central Statistics Office (1995) and the Connell projections indicate that the elderly population will exceed 600,000 persons by the year 2021, with the CSO projecting an elderly population of almost 700,000 persons by the year 2026 (National Council for the Elderly 1996:3–4).

Because the elderly are now representing an increasingly growing group in society, distinctions have been made, and we now refer to the elderly as:

1. the 'younger elderly' (sixty-five to seventy-five years)
2. the 'older elderly' (seventy-five to eighty-five years)
3. the very old (eighty-six years and over). (Macionis and Plummer 2002:329)

On average, people live to much older ages than was true over a century ago. Underlying this gain in lifespan are medical advances and improvements in nutrition, hygiene and health care. Some sociologists refer to the changing demographics of the elderly as the 'greying of the population'. 'Nearly all developed countries will witness the ageing of their populations in the next decades' (Giddens 2001:163). Peter Peterson 'has described this shift as a "gray down"' (1999, cited in Giddens 2001:163). According to his findings:

1. One in every seven people in the developed world is aged over sixty-five.
2. In thirty years' time, this will have risen to one in four.
3. By 2030, the proportion of people over sixty-five will range from thirty-three per cent in Australia to almost fifty per cent in Germany.
4. The number of the 'old old' (those aged over 85) is expanding more quickly than the 'young old'. Over the next half century, the number of

people over eighty-five will grow six-fold. This process is sometimes referred to as the 'ageing of the aged'. (Giddens 2001:163)

There are three reasons why sociologists need to consider old age more fully than they do at present:

1. Demographic factors: 'The role of demographic factors could be very significant on the size of the population pool in need of social care services such as personal care, home help and surveillance' (O'Loughlin 1999:235).
2. Ageing as an important social process in its own right.
3. Ageing as a key feature in class, gender or ethnic experience. (Webb and Tossell 1999:199)

'Across the world the expectation that people will live longer, and that an increasing proportion of the population will be older, is having repercussions on demographic, economic, medical and social frameworks' (Marsh 2000:545). As the elderly population continues to grow, the demands on social services and health systems will increase as well. As the old-age dependency ratio groups grow, increasing strain will be placed on available resources. Pensions will need to be paid for more years than they are at present. 'In the light of demographic projections, governments, interest groups and policy makers are being forced to look ahead and to develop proposals for meeting the needs of a changing population' (Giddens 2001:163). Gerontology, the study of ageing and the elderly, concerns itself not only with the physical process of growing old, but also with social and cultural factors connected with ageing.

1. Physical process of ageing: 'The ageing process starts at birth and slowly begins to accelerate when we are in our late twenties when the first physical signs such as greying hair or facial lines begin to show, and early aches and pains start to establish' (Webb and Tossell 1999:198). However, by the time we reach old age, most of us are psychologically adjusted to cope and have accustomed to having to 'live with a gradual diminishing physical capacity' (*Ibid.*:198). For Cole, 'growing old is a chronological and biological fact. The body changes with age, and death is an eventuality that none of us escape, but these simple truths tell us little of the social experience of old age' (1999:71).

2. Social process of ageing: Sociologists say that old age, like age in general, is socially constructed. In contemporary industrial societies, old age is defined by reference to retirement. For Cole, 'This experience of old age is a social one because it is society that defines what it is to be old and what meaning, expectations and status are attached to it' (1999:71). Some elderly people have commented that their advancing years have no effect on how they see themselves, but have changed the way in which other people have related to them. (Bilton *et al.* 2002:86)

An experiment conducted in New York over a three-year period highlights 'the fact that elders within a society are handicapped not so much by their psychological disabilities as by the attitudes and psychological barriers that are set up by other people' (Webb and Tossell 1999:199).

Ageing is not a uniformly experienced phenomenon. While there are examples of older people living well into their eighties and nineties and living full and active lives, ageing is also accompanied by a set of unfamiliar challenges. The elderly in our society remain 'largely on the periphery, unable in many cases to enjoy the benefits of a developed society to which they have all made contributions' (Webb and Tossell 1999:198).

TRANSITIONS AND PROBLEMS OF AGEING

A lot of problems and challenges experienced by the elderly are very much compounded by society's attitudes towards them. Webb and Tossell believe that the use of terms such as 'pensioner', 'geriatric' etc., words commonly used in association with elders, 'help to perpetuate the stereotyped image of their dependency and perceived uselessness, and so deny their human validity' (1999:199). Among the problems of the elderly are loss of role (resulting largely from retirement), loss of relatives and friends, separation from children who live elsewhere, poverty as a result of unemployment, etc.

'Older people in modern societies tend to have lower status and less power than they used to have in pre-modern cultures. In these cultures, as in non-Western societies today (such as India or China), old age was believed to bring wisdom, and the oldest people in any given community were commonly its main decision-makers. Today, increasing age normally brings with it something of the reverse . . . the accumulated knowledge of older people often seems to the young no longer a valuable store of wisdom, but simply behind the times' (Giddens 2001:162).

'Because our culture places such a premium on youth, ageing may spark frustration, fear and self-doubt' (Hamel 1990, cited in Macionis and Plummer 2002:329).

Retirement

'Retirement itself is a product of a wage-labour society, and more specifically of one where there is provision for income when employment has ceased, i.e. pensions' (Cole 1999:71).

Although the idea of retirement is familiar to us and seen as a socially acceptable period in which state and/or private pension provision is made, it is actually a recent creation, becoming commonplace in industrial societies during the nineteenth century. Retirement pensions were first introduced in 1899 by the German Chancellor Otto Von Bismarck. At the time the age set was seventy but was lowered to sixty-five in 1916 (Macionis and Plummer 2002:331). Retirement 'offered those who left the labour market a legitimate role as an ex-worker' (Bilton *et al.* 2002:87).

In Ireland, the old age Pension Act was introduced in 1908, but this was a strictly means-tested pension for people over seventy years old. The 1960s saw the introduction of the Contributory Old Age Pension (1961) (Mills 1999:6/7). The pension age was reduced from seventy to sixty-six by 1977. In 1970 a retirement pension for those at age sixty-five began (O'Loughlin 1999:225). 'As the pattern of work changes in industrial societies, so there is a pronounced tendency for people to retire at earlier and earlier ages – sometimes by choice, sometimes through compulsory redundancies' (Macionis and Plummer 2002:331).

Reasons for this could include the following:

- It allows more 'younger workers', who may have more up-to-date skills, access to the labour force.
- Sophisticated technology may reduce the need for everyone to work, but requires that those who do have the relevant skills and training.
- Lowering of retirement ages could be linked to growth of unemployment.

Kennedy in *Ireland in the Coming Times* suggests 'that the National Pensions Board (NPB) estimates did not take sufficient account of the improvement in mortality over the past decade' (1997:148). She states 'The National Pensions Board made projections of the cost of social welfare pensions between 1990 and 2035 in 1990 prices. The cost projections were based on lower population estimates of those aged 65 years and over than the 1995 CSO projections used in this paper' (1997:148).

Private and public pensions provide an economic foundation for retirement. In some poor societies, where no pension schemes exist, 'most people work until they become incapacitated' (Macionis and Plummer 2002:331).

The move from working life to retirement is not an easy one and it can pose some problems for many older people. 'Retirement is likely to be particularly hard for those for whom work was an important source of social status, identity, and, most importantly, independence' (Turner 1993, cited in

Bilton *et al.* 2002:87). Work is important in our personal identity; it gives us a purpose in life.

Exiting the labour market through retirement can lead to many feeling socially excluded, socially isolated as well as experiencing a significant drop in their living standards. 'Overall, the elderly tend to be more materially disadvantaged than other segments of the population. Retirement results in a loss of income that may cause a significant drop in elderly people's standard of living' (Giddens 2001:165).

Bilton *et al.* state that 'the differing experience of the impact of retirement tends to reflect differences between the incomes that older people take with them to retirement' (2002:87). For Blaikie (1999) 'working-class retirement may often lack "an active concept of retirement" whereas middle-class retirement – with better resources – has led to an expanding consumer market and culture' (cited in Macionis and Plummer 2002:331).

In our society, fewer women than men have faced the transition of retirement, but this trend continues to change as the proportion of women in the labour force continues to rise.

'The pensions upon which the retired depend have become more unequal than in the past, in that many new pensioners enjoy higher levels of support via private or employment-related pensions' (Bilton *et al.* 2002:87). A result of this is an increase in income inequalities among pensioners which 'points to the need for us to differentiate among older people themselves as much as between them and younger generations' (*Ibid.*).

Social isolation

'For many people, growing old can be a time of social withdrawal and loss – loss of job, income, health, independence, role, status, friends and relatives. It is unsurprising that this can be a period of loneliness and social isolation' (Marsh 2000:545).

Potential isolation and loneliness can be a result of:

1. retirement cutting the older person off from friends and workmates
2. loss of status as a result of retirement; loneliness and disorientation; having to restructure the daily routine
3. death of spouse, partner may leave an older person on their own
4. limited physical mobility preventing the older person from meeting others
5. the decline of the extended family resulting in many old people living

isolated lives, either independently or surrounded only by their peers in old people's homes (O'Donnell 2002:229).

The following figures from the 2002 census provide details on the number of elderly living alone in Ireland.

Table 9:3 The Elderly Population: Numbers Living Alone by Age Group

	Aged 65 years and over	Aged 70 years and over	Aged 75 years and over
Persons	113,826	88,411	59,794
Males	38,014	27,169	16,974
Females	75,812	61,242	42,820

(Source: Census 2002 CSO)

The problem of social isolation falls heavily on women, who typically outlive their husbands. Life expectancy rates at birth for Ireland were 75.1 years for men and 80.3 years for women in 2001–3 (Census 2000:14). The census of 2002 provides us with statistics that show for the age group seventy-five and over, 35.18 per cent of women live alone, compared to 23.2 per cent of men (2002:63). 'As with everything to do with old age, it is strongly structured by gender' (Arber and Ginn 1995, cited in Macionis and Plummer 2002:333).

Macionis and Plummer (2002:332) point out that living alone is not the equivalent of feeling lonely. They use a survey from Walker and Maltby (1997) to illustrate this point:

Table 9:4 Old and Lonely: Proportion of Older People Who Often Feel Lonely by Country (%)

% feeling lonely often	Country
<5	Denmark
5–9	Germany, The Netherlands, UK
10–14	Belgium, France, Ireland, Luxembourg, Spain
15–19	Italy
20 or more	Portugal, Greece (36%)

(Source: adapted from Walker and Maltby 1997, cited in Macionis and Plummer 2003:332)

Fear of crime is another factor that tends to strand large numbers of old people in their own homes.

Our society values people who work because they can contribute to the wealth of a nation. Despite the fact that many of the elderly population did work in the past, they lack the purpose attributed to those who continue to do so. 'In this way elders share a common status with others who are unemployed' (Webb and Tossell 1999:200).

Poverty and inequalities

Lack of money is a major problem faced by many older people. Retirement results in a loss of income that may cause a significant drop in elderly people's standard of living.

According to Tovey and Share (2000:130), 'Poverty in Ireland is found decreasingly among the retired or elderly and increasingly among the unemployed (and consequently families with children). This contrasts with the situation in some other EU countries where the retired make up a much larger proportion of those in poverty, as do those in work – the "working poor".'

The true extent of poverty among the elderly may be difficult to detect. It may remain hidden from view. According to Macionis and Plummer, there are a number of reasons for this:

1. Personal pride – many elderly people may conceal their financial problems even from their own families, in the desire to maintain the dignity of independent living.
2. Admitting to having financial difficulties may be admitting that they can no longer provide for themselves. (2002:334)

Abuse of the elderly

Elder abuse or 'granny battering' has recently been identified as a problem by researchers, although the extent of the problem is difficult to estimate because, like violence against women and children, many victims are reluctant to talk about it. But it is an area that requires considerable attention because 'as the proportion of elderly people rises so does the incidence of abuse' (Holmstrom 1994, cited in Macionis and Plummer 2002:333).

Abuse of older people can take many forms, from passive neglect to active torment – which includes verbal, emotional, financial and physical harm (Macionis and Plummer 2002:333).

Recent evidence highlighted in the media over the last year has brought the public's attention to the need to protect our old. While abuse of the elderly may seem unreal, we have to look at how certain arrangements in society can contribute to it. Often the cause lies in the stress of caring – financially and emotionally – for ageing parents. 'Today's middle-aged adults represent a "sandwich generation" who may well spend as much time caring for their ageing parents as for their own children' (Macionis and Plummer 2002:333).

Ageism and discrimination

'Ageism is a set of beliefs originating in the biological variation between people and relating to the ageing process' (Bytheway 1995, cited in O'Loughlin 1999:222).

Ageism is prejudice and discrimination against the elderly. Whether we admit it or not, there is a tendency in society to regard 'older people as out of step with the youth-orientated consumer society' (Bilton *et al.* 2002:88).

Ageism distances older people from mainstream culture and generates a fear of the ageing process. It does so by providing stereotypes regarding the competence and need for protection by the elderly. Just like racism or sexism it can be blatant or subtle. It can be manifest in many ways. For example:

1. An older person may be refused a job because of their age. It is often believed that older workers are less competent than younger ones.
2. Elder abuse (highlighted above). Biggs (1999) argues that 'professional staff have the same negative stereotypes of the elderly as those found in the wider culture. They may also give priority to the organisational demands of the institution in which they work, rather than to the individual needs of its residents, resulting in ill-treatment or neglect' (cited in Bilton *et al.* 2002:88).

Activist groups have started to fight against ageism and are seeking to encourage a positive view of old age and older people. 'There is a certain lack of understanding about the status of older people in Irish society. Challenging the power of ageism will require facing the reality that it is a shared experience and seeing ourselves in terms of the broader context of the whole of our lives' (O'Loughlin 1999:235).

Death and dying

'Ireland's death statistics (mortality) now mirror those of other relatively affluent countries . . . In regard to lowering premature mortality (death before 65 years), Ireland trails behind other EU member states' (Quin 1999:28).

Despite the fact that we all die, modern society tries to foster 'eternal youth' by separating life from death. 'Death is physically removed from everyday activities' (Macionis and Plummer 2002:536). In the past people died at home in the presence of family and friends; today most deaths occur in hospitals, nursing homes or hospices. According to Ariès, 'Even hospitals commonly relegate dying patients to a special part of the building, and hospital morgues are located well out of sight of patients and visitors alike' (1974, cited in Macionis and Plummer 2002:536).

Bereavement

'A most devastating form of stress experienced by individuals is bereavement – a state characterised by loss' (Clarke *et al.* 2000:145). The intensity and experience of grief is unique for everyone, but studies suggest that most people experience a number of stages. According to some researchers, bereavement parallels the stages of dying described by Elisabeth Kübler-Ross (1969, cited in Macionis and Plummer 2002:537). The five stages she identified are:

1. anger
2. denial
3. negotiation
4. resignation
5. acceptance.

'All experts agree that how family and friends view a death influences the attitudes of the person who is dying. Specifically acceptance by others of the approaching death helps the dying person do the same. Denial of the impending death may isolate the dying person, who is then unable to share feelings and experiences with others' (Macionis and Plummer 2002:537).

The increase in the population of older people is going to have a significant influence on many aspects of Irish life. Statistics on the elderly show that there is both a need and a demand for health and social care services over the coming decades. The problems and challenges older people face today; ageism, abuse, poverty, should give us a sense of real concern. Failure to identify and confront these problems means they will become ours one day.

10

Race and Ethnicity

CHAPTER OBJECTIVES
After reading this chapter you should be able to:
• define race and ethnicity
• define prejudice
• define discrimination
• discuss racism and ethnic relations in Ireland – a case in point: Travellers.

RACE AND ETHNICITY DEFINED

Race

'Race usually refers to a category of people sharing biologically transmitted traits' (Macionis and Plummer 2002:259).

The word 'race' came into the English language at the beginning of the sixteenth century. When it was used at that time, it was used simply to refer to groups of people connected by common origin. It was used loosely to refer to likenesses or similarities of people of shared descent (Mann 1983). The concept of race took on a whole new meaning in the eighteenth and nineteenth centuries. During this period the scientific theories of 'race' arose and it took on a different, more dangerous meaning. 'Peoples of the world – within and beyond Europe – were being classified and ranked into superior and inferior races with allegedly inherent capacities and characteristics' (Bilton *et al.* 2002:162). Beliefs about the different capacities of distinct races offered an explanation and justification for the ruling powers such as England and other European countries to exercise control over colonies and their people.

Count Joseph Arthur de Gobineau (1816–82), who is sometimes called the father of modern racism, proposed the existence of three races:

1. white (Caucasian)
2. black (Negroid)

3. yellow (Mongoloid).

According to Giddens, Gobineau believed that 'the white race possesses superior intelligence, morality and will-power, it is these inherited qualities that underlie the spread of Western influence across the world. The blacks, by contrast, are the least capable, marked by an animal nature, a lack of morality and emotional instability' (2001:245). Scientific ideas about racial difference continued to have a significant impact in the twentieth century. They influenced Hitler and the Nazi party, the Ku-Klux Klan in the US and the architects of apartheid in South Africa and have cost the lives of millions of people.

Superficial differences between people do exist. We do have different skin colour, facial features, hair texture, etc. These superficial differences 'are nothing more than indicators of how the human race has adapted to its various climatic surroundings during the evolutionary process' (Webb and Tossell 1999:82). Since the end of World War II 'race science' has been thoroughly discredited. Scientists today are continuing to challenge the links between biology and behaviour that had underpinned earlier beliefs. According to Donohoe and Gaynor (1999:100) 'in the biological/ physiological sense it is not possible to divide human groups according to race'. The results of an international study, the 'human genome' project, were published in 2001. They indicated 'that every person on earth shares 99.99% of their genetic code with all other people. There is no separate Jewish race or Irish race. There is no evidence of racial differences in intelligence that could not equally be accounted for by environmental factors' (O'Donnell 2002:249). We are all members of a single biological species, we are all members of the human race.

Migration and intermarriage over the course of human history means that people the world over display a bewildering array of racial traits. 'No society lacks genetic mixture, and increasing contact among the world's people will ensure that racial blending will accelerate in the future (Macionis and Plummer 2002:259).

However, the term 'race' remains a powerful social concept which is widely understood and used. For Bilton et al., 'Race remains a potent basis for identity – our sense of sameness and difference' (2002:164). In social life nineteenth-century ideas about racial characters are still used by members of powerful groups to set at a distance members of weaker groups. According to Bilton et al., some social scientists wish to focus on ethnic differences as opposed to racial differences. To forget or ignore the concept of race would be in a way like ignoring the millions who have suffered or died because of it (and who continue to do so). To avoid this some scholars therefore 'choose to use the word "race" in inverted commas to reflect its misleading, but commonplace usage' (Giddens 2001:246).

Ethnicity

'Ethnic group is used to describe groups of people who share common cultural characteristics, for example, language, dress, food, religion, customs, beliefs and traditions' (Donohoe and Gaynor 1999:101).

'Ethnicity is used in ethnic relations literature to refer to a sense of cultural awareness and identity within groups that share a common history or heritage' (Marsh 2000:391).

According to Mann, the first recorded use of the word 'ethnicity' dates from 1953 (1983:114). The word itself derives from the Greek word 'ethnos' meaning 'a people'. Ethnicity is sometimes confused with race, but while the two can sometimes go hand in hand, it is important to make a distinction between them. Race has a firm sense of biological difference while ethnicity relies on cultural heritage (Macionis and Plummer 2002).

To qualify as an ethnic group, a group must fulfil the following objective scientific criteria:

1. they must be biologically self-perpetuating
2. they must be racially different
3. they must share fundamental cultural values and cultural difference
4. they must be socially separated from other groups
5. language barriers must be present
6. they must be self-ascribed and externally ascribed
7. they must show signs of organised and spontaneous enmity (Ní Shuinéar 1996:55–59).

'Members of ethnic groups see themselves as culturally distinct from other groups in a society, and are seen by those other groups to be so in return' (Giddens 2001:246). People in ethnic groups see themselves and are seen by others as having a distinct identity. Their ethnicity is central to the individual and group identity. In Ireland, the Travellers are an ethnic group as are the different groups of refugees from various countries (Donohoe and Gaynor 1999:101).

PREJUDICE

'Prejudice is defined as hostile or negative attitudes based on ignorance and faulty or incomplete knowledge. It is characterised by a tendency to stereotype, that is a tendency to assign identical characteristics to whole groups regardless of individual variations' (Twitchin *et al.*, cited in Rattansi 1992:25).

Prejudice is difficult to define and can take many forms. Weber states that 'Prejudice is acquired through learning, as part of normal socialisation and in developing social identity through group membership' (cited in MacGreil 1996:18).

The following list highlights some of the key characteristics of prejudice:

1. It is an attitude – a prejudgment.
2. Prejudices can be positive or negative.
3. Prejudices are irrational. They are not based on reasonable, factual evidence. They are usually based on hearsay.
4. Prejudice is based on fear.
5. Prejudices are based on a lack of knowledge.

Gordon Allport, a leading authority on social prejudice, identified the following five progressively severe stages of behaviour that could result if social prejudice was acted out and not corrected:

Stage 1:   Antilocution or ridicule
Stage 2:   Avoidance or shunning
Stage 3:   Discrimination
Stage 4:   Physical attack
Stage 5:   Extermination or expulsion. (Allport 1954, cited in MacGreil 1996:21)

Whether we acknowledge it or admit it, we all have prejudices. In almost all societies, if not in all, each new generation of people is taught 'appropriate' beliefs regarding other groups. People commonly hold prejudices (negative or positive) about individuals of a particular race, ethnicity, class, sexual orientation and so on. 'Our positive prejudices tend to exaggerate the virtues of people like ourselves, while our negative prejudices condemn those who differ from us' (Macionis and Plummer 2002:261). Prejudice is most often applied by the more powerful in society, by those with authority and influence, to the less powerful; 'whatever its cause, an ignorance of those to whom it is directed is nearly always present' (Webb and Tossell 1999:16).

DISCRIMINATION

'Discrimination means policies, practices or behaviour which leads to the unfair treatment of individuals or groups because of their identity or their perceived identity' (Donohoe and Gaynor 2003:64).

Discrimination is the expression of prejudice; it is a matter of behaviour, for example denying Travellers access to bars and restaurants, etc. When we speak of discrimination we are referring to any action that involves treating categories of people unequally. Common types of discrimination include:

1. age
2. class
3. culture
4. gender
5. health status
6. HIV status
7. marital status
8. cognitive ability
9. mental health
10. offending background
11. physical ability
12. place of origin
13. political beliefs
14. race
15. religion
16. responsibility for dependants
17. sensory ability
18. sexuality. (Clarke *et al.* 2000:19–21)

Discrimination can be subtle or blatant but either way the effect of it on an individual can be serious. Those who experience discrimination can feel rejected and powerless and it can result in loss of their self-esteem and confidence.

Unfortunately, the problem of discrimination is extensive and results in inequality in access to services and the disqualification of members of one group from opportunities open to others. The most damaging form of discrimination is 'Institutional discrimination – which refers to bias in attitudes or action inherent in the operation of society's institutions, including schools, hospitals, the police and the workplace' (Macionis and Plummer 2002:267). An analysis of a society's health and social problems would show a truer picture of the extent of institutional discrimination in operation in our society. As a society we must learn to tackle intolerance, the problem that links all forms of discrimination. 'It is not unusual to be suspicious of those not like us in appearance, beliefs, background and much more. the real challenge in developing anti-discriminatory practice in the caring services is to develop a more tolerant attitude to differences between people' (Clarke *et al.* 2000:19).

Fighting intolerance means fighting fear.

RACISM AND ETHNIC RELATIONS IN IRELAND: A CASE IN POINT – TRAVELLERS

'Racism equals prejudice plus power. In other words, racism is a combination of individual racial prejudice and society's support' (Webb and Tossell 1999:82). The roots of racism are to be found in the past, at a time when it was used to justify the African slave trade and the system of imperialism. Its underlying belief was that one racial category was innately superior or inferior to another and thereby the superior group had right to dominance. 'Although the term race has a long history, the term racism only entered common usage after the Second World War as a way of describing the horrors of the Holocaust' (Bilton *et al.* 2002:178).

Racism remains a widespread and serious social problem. Despite attempts to dispel the notion that inferiority and superiority can be justified by skin colour or physiognomy, racism is still extensive. Scientists now refer to 'New racism (or cultural racism) which uses the idea of cultural differences to exclude certain groups' (Barker 1981, cited in Giddens 2001:252). New racism implies that discrimination is now experienced by individuals or groups not because of their biological differences but because of their cultural arrangements. Those groups in a society that stand apart from the majority can 'become marginalized or vilified for their refusal to assimilate' (Giddens 2001:252).

'The fact that racism is increasingly exercised on cultural rather than biological grounds has led some scholars to suggest that we live in an age of "multiple racisms" where discrimination is experienced differently across segments of the population' (Modood *et al.* 1997).

Racism is more than simply the ideas of a few racist individuals; it is much more deep-seated than that. It is embedded in the very structure of our society. Institutional racism is rife, 'the practices and procedures of so many of our organisations are consciously or unconsciously racist in that they operate unfavourably towards, and therefore discriminate against people from ethnic minorities' (Webb and Tossell 1999:82). The following example will show how institutions such as the health service, the educational system, etc., all promote policies that favour certain groups while discriminating against others.

Travellers and racism in Ireland

'Travellers are widely acknowledged as one of the most marginalized and disadvantaged groups in Irish society. Travellers fare poorly on every indicator used to measure disadvantage: unemployment, poverty, social exclusion, health status, infant mortality, life expectancy, illiteracy, education and training levels, access to decision-making and political representation, gender equality, access to credit, accommodation and living conditions. The circumstances of the Irish Travelling people are intolerable. No humane and decent society, once made aware of such circumstances, could permit them to persist' (ESRI July 1986, cited in National Co-ordinating Committee for European Year against Racism 1997).

Travellers are an ethnic minority group who make up approximately 0.5 per cent of the population of Ireland. According to Census 2002: 'There are 23,681 Travellers nationally' (cited in www.nccri.com). Travellers as a group have a long history (dating back to the twelfth century), and an identity marked by a number of common characteristics – an oral tradition, their own language, etc. Travellers can be considered an 'ethnic group because they regard themselves and are regarded by others as a distinct community by virtue of the following characteristics' (Kenny, cited in Centre for Gypsy Research 1992:171):

1. They have a long, shared history.
2. They have their own values, customs, lifestyles and traditions associated with nomadism.
3. They come from a small number of ancestors . . . one becomes a Traveller not just by choice but by birth.
4. They have their own language called Cant, Gammon or Sheltie and are also recognisable by their accents and use of language.
5. They have an oral tradition rich in folklore and also have a distinctive style of singing.
6. The majority adhere to a form of popular religiosity in the Roman Catholic tradition (Centre for Gypsy Research 1992:17). '21,549 Travellers identified themselves as Roman Catholic' (Census 2002, cited in www.nccri.com).

The Traveller community in Ireland experiences prejudice and social discrimination at all levels of society. Because they are a distinct and unique group, recognised by themselves and others, they face an ongoing struggle for survival. They face much opposition and pressure to conform to sedentary society; resistance to doing so means they experience low social status and exclusion 'which prevents them from participating as equals in society' (DTEDG 1992:4). The discrimination experienced by the Travelling community is a result of the widespread hostility and prejudice of the settled people/community towards them and it affects all aspects of their lives.

The following section will examine the effects of discrimination on Travellers in relation to the following:

1. general lifestyle
2. health
3. accommodation
4. education
5. economy.

General discrimination

'Research into the living circumstances of Irish Travellers shows that they are: a uniquely disadvantaged group, impoverished, under-educated, often despised and ostracised, they live on the margins of Irish society' (ESRI 1986, cited in MacLaughlin 1995:27). Although Travellers experience prejudice and discrimination in Irish society, there is an unwillingness among the Irish public to acknowledge this behaviour as racist. Two key reasons have been identified for this:

1. People still equate racism with skin colour. It is frequently said 'that Travellers cannot experience racism because they are white, are not a different "race" nor a different nationality' (National Co-ordinating Committee for European Year against Racism 1997:6).
2. There is also a tendency for Irish people to deny that racism exists in our country and in themselves. According to the Committee (1997:6), Ireland is not unique in this context; it goes on to say that 'the forms of prejudice and discrimination experienced by the Travelling community equates with racism in the international context'.

The ethnic status of the Traveller community has been contested by the majority settled community. Travellers and their way of life are seen as the problem. According to Noonan, 'Those who do not accept Travellers as an ethnic group have usually inverted this relationship and have viewed Travellers from a pathological perspective which blames them as "deviants", "drop-outs", "failed settled people" or a culture of poverty' (1996:170). Crowley (1999:244) believes that such definitions of Travellers denies them as a people with their own history, culture, etc., and instead sees them as a people in need of rehabilitation and assimilation. Such beliefs need to be examined and analysed against a tradition which:

1. 'Prioritised sedentarism over nomadism and
2. which legitimised the social and cultural values of settled communities and property-owners while undermining the position of the propertyless' (MacLaughlin 1995:27).

Travellers are often viewed as scroungers and thieves, while the use of terms like 'knackers' and 'itinerants' debases Travellers to the level of a racial minority. The level of racism (individual and institutional) and the degree of anti-Traveller exclusion is very high. A survey carried out by the Irish Traveller Movement in 1994 provided the following results:

1. Eight out of ten Travellers were refused service in a pub.
2. Five out of ten Travellers were asked to leave a shop.
3. Three out of ten Travellers were asked to leave a hairdresser's.
4. Two out of ten Travellers were asked to leave a laundry. (McDonagh, cited in The Parish of the Travelling Community 2000:115)

MacGreil (1996:341) in his study *Prejudice in Ireland Revisited* refers to the Travelling peoples as Ireland's apartheid. In this study, 1988–9, he tried to gauge how close settled people were willing to get with the Travelling community. It then compared the results of this study with the results of a similar one carried out in 1972–3. 'The findings were surprisingly negative and show a substantial deterioration in the Dublin sample since 1972–73':

• Only one in seven of the national sample would welcome a Traveller into the family through marriage.
• Fifty-nine per cent (three out of five) would not welcome Travellers as next-door neighbours.
• One in ten would deny citizenship to Irish Travellers. (MacGreil 1996:327)

The following remarks made by a Fianna Fáil councillor at a Waterford County Council meeting (cited in National Co-ordinating Committee for European Year against Racism 1997:9) highlights the extent of the last finding: 'The sooner the shotguns are at the ready and these Travelling people are put out of our country the better. They are not our people, they aren't natives.'

On further examination of research findings, MacGreil found that 'way of life' was the dominant reason for not welcoming Travellers into the family (seventy-seven per cent). One-fifth of the respondents gave 'not socially acceptable' as their main reason. MacGreil concluded that 'the Irish people's prejudices against the Travellers is one of caste-like apartheid' (1996:341).

Anti-Traveller racism in Ireland is rooted in a belief that the way of life of settled people is the norm. This ideology is at the root of the social, economic and geographical exclusion of Travellers from Irish society. According to Donohoe and Gaynor, most of the difficulties and problems experienced by Travellers 'are caused not by ignorance and lack of education on the part of the Traveller, but by ignorance, prejudice, discrimination and lack of education on the part of the settled community' (2003:79). The following statistics on Traveller health, education and accommodation provide very graphic evidence of the extent of institutional racism towards them in our society.

Traveller health

'Travellers are only now reaching the life expectancy that settled Irish people achieved in the 1940s' (Barry *et al.* 1987, cited in Task Force on the Travelling Community 1995:135).

Statistics on the health status of the Travelling community in Ireland provide evidence of the harsh reality of the intolerable living conditions of the majority of the Traveller population. The last comprehensive statistical analysis of Traveller health took place in 1987. This study, 'The Travellers Health Status Study' (Barry *et al.* 1989) found that 'the infant mortality rate for Travellers in 1987 was 18.1 per 1000 live births compared to the national figure of 7.4' (cited in Crowley 1999:244).

Studies of Travellers' health status when compared to that of the settled community show that:

- Still births are twice as likely among Travellers.
- Traveller children are three times more likely to be hospitalised in the first year of life.
- Men's life expectancy is ten years less, women's is twelve years less than that of settled people; in the settled community women tend to live longer than men, but in the Traveller community this is reversed.
- In all age groups Travellers have higher mortality rates.
- More Travellers than settled people die due to:
  - accidents
  - respiratory problems
  - congenital problems
  - metabolic disorders in the 0–14 year age group.
  (Donohoe and Gaynor 2003:77)

According to the 2002 census (cited in www.nccri), only 3.3 per cent of the Traveller population are over sixty-five years of age. Poor living conditions, social exclusion and racism are the main cause of Travellers' inferior health status. Another contributing factor is the failure of health services to meet and adapt to their specific needs. For Fanning, 'in particular they [health services] have not adequately responded to Traveller culture and how it may shape perceptions of and responses to ill health and services' (2002, cited in Tovey and Share 2003:285).

Traveller accommodation

In 1960, four per cent of Travellers were housed. By 1980 this figure was just under forty per cent. MacLaughlin's statistics illustrate how dramatically Traveller accommodation has changed in the twenty-year period between 1960 and 1980. His figures also show that in 1980:

- A further fifteen per cent of Travellers were living on serviced sites.
- Almost half of all Traveller families were still living on the roadside and that there were almost 300 Traveller families on the roadside in the Dublin area alone. (1995:27)

'The most recent count of Traveller families provides further evidence of institutional racism. It identified 1,127 families as living on the side of the road without basic facilities and subject to the constant threat of eviction. This figure is out of a total of 4,521 families identified in the count, which took place in 1997' (Crowley 1999:244).

Travellers live in the following types of accommodation:

1. standard housing (in mixed housing schemes)
2. group housing schemes (all Travellers)
3. official halting sites – permanent sites have full services, temporary ones often do not
4. unofficial halting sites (on the roadside). This accounts for about thirty-five per cent of Traveller accommodation. (Donohoe and Gaynor 2003:78)

Donohoe and Gaynor refer to a survey by the Dublin Accommodation Coalition for Travellers which highlights the appalling living conditions of some of these Travellers:

- Sixteen per cent of Travellers had no water supply.
- Fifty-three per cent of Travellers had no electricity supply.
- Thirty-six per cent of Travellers had no toilet.
- Fifty-three per cent of Travellers had no bath or shower facilities.

- Ten per cent of Travellers had no rubbish collection. (2003:78)

Local authorities were required by the Housing (Traveller Accommodation) Act 1998 to draw up a five-year plan in relation to Traveller accommodation. Failure to address the needs of the Traveller community, to ignore their ethnicity by enforcing assimilationist policies, encourages anti-Traveller racism and heightens tensions between the Traveller and settled communities. As MacLaughlin (1995:80) states 'Local authorities often "hide" halting sites away from towns and cities and locate them in isolated areas away from shops, schools and community services. They particularly ignore Traveller preferences for small extended family sites and pay more attention to placating the majority population than addressing the needs of Travellers.'

Traveller education

The educational status of Travellers provides further evidence of racism. According to the Report of the Special Education Review Committee 1993 (cited in Crowley 1999:245), it was estimated that 'of the 5,000 Traveller children of primary school age, 4,200 were attending'. Donohoe and Gaynor provide the following information in relation to Traveller education:

1. About ninety per cent attend primary school.
2. More than half of these are segregated into special classes or schools.
3. Only twelve per cent continue into secondary school and a mere handful proceed to do the Leaving Cert. (2003:79)
4. Eighty per cent of adult Travellers are unable to read. (Dept of Health and Children 2002–05)

Two key reasons identified for lack of participation by the Traveller community in education are:

1. failure to address their distinct cultural identity and nomadic lifestyle, and
2. segregation in early childhood services and at primary level.

According to Kenny, 'improvement of the educational experience for Travellers depends on proactive change within schools: if education provision from the central policy-makers through to the local classrooms were informed by principles of anti-racism and inter-culturalism, the need for special support for Travellers would be pared back to its true extent, because at least an alien school programme would not be confounding the difficulties confronting Traveller children' (1997, cited in Tovey and Share 2003:223).

Traveller economy

Many Travellers live in poverty and depend on social welfare for survival. Up until the late twentieth century Travellers had an economy based on a range of activities such as tin-smithing, seasonal farming and recycling. However, with the increased use of materials such as plastic and machinery for repairs, their skills and occupations became obsolete and forced many of the population to move to urban areas. Many Travellers today try to remain self-employed by dealing in scrap and recycling but because this economy is marginalised, the majority of Travellers live in poverty' (Donohoe and Gaynor 2003:77).

Over the years, the government has made clear and explicit attempts to respond to Travellers' needs. Some of these attempts can be seen in:

- The Report of the Commission in Itinerancy, 1963
- The Report of the Travelling People Review Body, 1983
- The Report of the Task Force on the Travelling community, 1995.

Despite some progress made by these reports, much of the work done to highlight the plight of the Travelling community has been carried out by groups such as the Irish Travellers Movement, National Traveller Women's forum, Pavee Point Travellers Centre, etc. MacLaughlin views 'the upsurge of Traveller awareness groups under a leadership drawn from the Traveller community itself as [having] done much to redress the devaluation of Traveller culture, both by the settled community and more damagingly, by Travellers themselves' (1995:82).

The Traveller community suffers significant disadvantages in comparison to the general population. Travellers in Ireland experience the effects of ethnocentrism – 'the belief that one group of people's way of life is the best way to live and is the way every group should live, even if this way of life has to be forced on another group' (McDonagh, cited in The Parish of the Travelling Community 2000:116). The situation of the Travelling community reflects our ethnocentric and racist nature. 'Despite widespread and profound ignorance of traveller culture, most government and local authority departments have presumed to know what is best for Travellers' (Noonan 1996:173). We need to confront this ignorance and begin to acknowledge and appreciate the many varied and wonderful cultures around us. Easier said than done, but maybe the following challenge offered to us by Crowley will make us sit up and think: 'I would like to pose racism as a challenge to white people and settled people – both groups of which I am a member. White people and settled people benefit from a racist society – we are affirmed, we are resourced. As such we cannot be neutral – we can only be racist or anti-racist' (Crowley 1999:87).

11

Sociology of Health

CHAPTER OBJECTIVES

After reading this chapter you should be able to:
- define 'health'
- outline the social causes of illness
- understand what is meant by sociology of the body
- discuss the relationship between health and gender
- explain the social aspects of health.

HEALTH DEFINED

In its 1946 Constitution, the World Health Organization defined health as a 'state of complete physical, mental and social well-being' (Tovey and Share 2000:234). This definition of health sees it in a holistic way, and because of this problems arise. Tovey and Share suggest that few of us, if asked, could claim such an ideal and cite research by MacFarlane (1997) that reveals that up to '95% of the population experiences some sort of ill health in any two-week period'.

'Health status' is the term used to describe the present state of illness or wellness in a community. Doorley (1998:17) describes health status in terms of 'rates of death and illness in a community, the prevalence of good and poor health practices, rates of death and disease (chronic and infectious) and the prevalence of symptoms/conditions of well-being' (cited in Tovey and Share 2003:276).

Tovey and Share in their chapter 'The Body, Health and Illness' highlight that the most common indicators of health status are:

1. life expectancy
2. death rates
3. morbidity rates (rates of incidence of certain diseases)
4. patterns of lifestyle, and
5. self-perceived health (2003:276).

They believe that a lack of available information on these indicators at a local level has made it difficult to analyse health patterns in Ireland and as a result these have not informed policy-making in a critical way.

SOCIAL CAUSES OF ILLNESS

According to Bilton *et al.* (2002:358) 'The sociology of health and illness is concerned with the social origins and influences on disease rather than with exploring its organic manifestation in individual bodies.' Macionis and Plummer (2002:514) regard 'Health as much a social as a biological issue' and believe that it can tell us a lot about how a society works. Sociologists believe that you cannot ignore the important role of social and environmental influences on patterns of health and illness. 'The improvements in overall public health over the past century cannot conceal the fact that health and illness are not distributed evenly throughout the population' (Giddens 2001:144). Societies that tend to show large variations in levels of sickness and early deaths are likely to be organised very differently from those where people live longer and experience less illness (Macionis and Plummer 2002:514). Macionis and Plummer (2002) believe that the characteristics of the surrounding society shape the health of its population. For them, the key aspects of health include the following:

1. **People judge their health relative to others**: 'As standards of health vary from society to society, health is sometimes a matter of having the same diseases as one's neighbours' (2002:514).

2. **People often equate 'health' with morality**: Conformity to cultural norms is often encouraged by ideas about good health. According to Morgan *et al.*, homosexuality was classified as a disease until 1973 when the American Psychiatric Association voted that it no longer be seen as an illness (1983, cited in Bilton *et al.* 2002:438). 'Those who contract a sexually linked disease may be looked upon as morally suspect. Indeed some countries require potential immigrants to take HIV and syphilis tests before they are given visas' (Macionis and Plummer 2002:514).

3. **Cultural standards of health change over time**: 'People's perception of health and illness is culturally variable, highly context-specific, dynamic and subject to change' (Bilton *et al.* 2002:358). They give the example of suntan, which many associate with health and good looks, rather than leading to 'wrinkled skin or skin cancer'. The smoking ban in this country since 2004 shows how attitudes to smoking and its dangers have changed over the years.

4. Health and living standards are interrelated: High levels of infectious disease are found in poor societies that contend with malnutrition and poor sanitation. In Irish society, Traveller accommodation provision was criticised for 'Inadequate provision with one-quarter of families living on the side of the road without access to basic facilities' (Crowley 1999:250).

5. Health relates to social inequality: Certain groups of people tend to enjoy much better health than others. According to Giddens, 'health inequalities appear to be tied to larger socio-economic patterns' (2001:145). Balanda and Wilde (2001) reported that 'those in the "lowest" class are 15 times more likely to die from homicide, six times more likely to die from respiratory disease, and seventeen times more likely to die of alcoholism' (cited in Tovey and Share 2003:284). Activities such as smoking, poor diet and higher consumption of alcohol, which are detrimental to good health, tend to be higher among the lower social classes. This argument sees individuals as bearing primary responsibility for poor health, as many lifestyles are freely made (Giddens 2001:147).

SOCIOLOGY OF THE BODY

The field known as sociology of the body is relatively new. Sociologists in this area investigate the ways in which our bodies are affected by social influences. 'Our bodies are deeply affected by our social experiences, as well as by the norms and values of the groups to which we belong. It is only recently that sociologists have begun to recognise the profound nature of the interconnections between social life and the body' (Giddens 2001:144).

Interest in the social importance of the body has been 'stimulated by a number of factors' (Nettleson and Watson 1998, cited in Tovey and Share 2003:270). These factors include:

1. a politicisation of the body
2. demographic change
3. rise in consumer culture
4. the development of new technologies
5. the development of communications technologies.

Feminists and disabled groups have played a big part in the politicisation of the body. Feminists focus on how women's bodies have been controlled and abused in a range of cultures, for example, analysis of childbirth and eating disorders has highlighted the role of advertising and the medical industry in this control and abuse. Disabled groups on the other hand focus on how society discriminates against those who do not fit in with the dominant view of the 'normal' body.

People are now living longer and this has led to new issues such as the quality of life in later years. A rise in the consumer culture means that people are now spending more on cosmetics, fashion, surgery, etc. Adele Clarke (1995:147) estimates that plastic surgery is a '$1.75 billion a year industry in the US, with about 1.5 million people undergoing plastic surgery of some kind!' (cited in Macionis and Plummer 2002:170). The development of new technologies is also having a huge effect on our bodies. Boundaries between humans and new technology are questioned with the development of new surgical techniques such as organ transplants and cosmetic surgery. Finally, digital cameras, the internet, etc. have made it difficult to distinguish between the 'virtual' and the 'real'. 'In an age where a person can continuously retouch their own family photograph album, the physical body may become a touchstone of 'reality and authenticity' (Tovey and Share 2003:271).

Overall, people today are increasingly preoccupied with getting their bodies under control. Examples of this can be seen in people's preoccupation with diets, fitness regimes, etc. Sociologists studying 'the body' attempt to analyse 'how people view, use and feel about their bodies within a range of social settings and structural situations' (Tovey and Share 2003:271).

HEALTH AND GENDER

What is the relationship between health and gender? How does gender impact on health experience? Men and women do have specific conditions related to their genes and biological make-up, for example women experience childbirth and menstruation, testicular cancer is a condition specific to men. According to Marsh, 'the main differences in health experience, are related to the social construction of gender: that is, the ideas we, as a society, have about what is expected of men and women' (2000:477).

In Ireland, as in most other countries, health status is clearly patterned by gender. Statistics provided by the Department of Health in 1997 showed that 'while there had been much improvement since the middle of the century, women in Ireland have a lower life expectancy and a higher premature mortality rate than average' (cited in Quin 1999:39). These figures surrounding Irish women's health were looked at in the EU context and also highlighted a plight experienced by Traveller women 'who have a life expectancy of 12 years less than average, reflecting a lifestyle and service response that grossly neglects their needs' (Ibid. 1999:39).

Although women report more illness than men they live longer. Marsh believes that the increasing differences in mortality rates between male and female in the developed countries 'have been attributed to reduced rates of death in women from childbearing, and greater mortality in men from cardiovascular disease and cancers' (2000:478).

Research by Balanda and Wilde (2001, cited in Tovey and Share 2003:286), found that the following causes of death are more likely to apply to women in Ireland:

1. meningitis
2. congenital malformation of the nervous system
3. disease of the skin and of the musculo-skeletal system, such as rheumatoid arthritis and osteoarthrosis.

Mahon (1997), also cited Tovey and Share's *A Sociology of Ireland* (2003:286), has found that 'Irish women have rates of certain cancers (colon, breast, larynx and oesophagus) and ischaemic heart disease that are among the highest in the EU'.

Researchers are interested in attempting to answer questions on why women live longer than men. The following factors are considered:

1. **Biology**: Nathanson (1984) states that 'some researchers have suggested that the extra chromosome carried by women confers some protection, in part making them more resistant to disease in childhood' (cited in Marsh 2000:478).

2. **Behaviour**: Do men take more risks than women? Are they more likely to take part in dangerous sports or violent activities? Eurostat (1995, cited in Macionis and Plummer 2002:523) reported that violent deaths as a result of suicides and accidents are the single most important cause of death amongst young men between fifteen and twenty-four in the EU (as elsewhere). The suicide rate for males has also increased sharply in Ireland and other western societies. Statistics presented by Balanda and Wilde state that 'Irish males are now nearly four times more likely to end their own lives than females' (2001, cited in Tovey and Share 2003:286). Alcohol-related activities are also higher among men. Marsh suggests that this could be related to the fact that drinking alcohol is a 'more socially acceptable response to stress for men than it is for women' (2000:479).

3. **Social and environmental**: Are men socialised to behave in more 'risk-taking' ways?

4. **The use of health services**: According to Waldron, 'women tend to consult doctors more often and may be more likely to use preventative health services. However, for most major causes of mortality, there appear

to be few differences in the use of curative medicine' (1985, cited in Marsh 2000:478). Higher rates of GP visits could be due to their role within the family and their responsibility for family health or to the fact that women are more socialised to accept health.

'Women in industrialised countries report twice as much anxiety and depression as men. The overall picture of women's health in the developed world is one in which women live longer than men, but are sicker and experience more disability' (Doyal, cited in Giddens 2001:148).

Developing a Policy for Women's Health (1995) was a discussion document that covered a range of areas relating to women's health. Areas covered included childbirth, breast and cancer screening and family planning. The aim was the development of a woman-friendly service.

It also addressed the area of women's participation in the formulation and management of health services as well as identifying women who were particularly disadvantaged in terms of health needs and/or access to an appropriate range of health services (Quin 1999:39).

Attempts continue to be made by sociologists of health and illness to account for gender-based disparities in health status. For Tovey and Share, 'Women's health issues are very much constructed as a matter of attitude, rather than structural inequality' (2003:287).

SOCIAL ASPECTS OF HEALTH

Social care

Class position has a huge impact on one's health status. One of the most important studies to look at health inequalities was the Black Report (1980) (updated in 1992 as the *Health Divide*). This study was carried out in the UK and one of its most shocking findings was 'that the child of an unskilled manual worker will die around 7 years earlier than a counterpart born to professional parents' (Macionis and Plummer 2002:521).

'Research has consistently indicated (for example Balanda and Wilde, 2001) that in advanced industrial economies like Ireland, the UK, Australia and the US, poor health status is associated with variation in social class' (Tovey and Share 2003:284). Tovey and Share list health factors (negative factors) associated with poorer and less powerful groups. These include higher levels of:

1. perinatal mortality
2. admission to psychiatric hospitals
3. standardised mortality rates

4. incidences of diseases such as pneumonia, cancer and heart disease
5. deaths from accidents, suicide and homicide. (2003:284)

Although there is a trend towards better health the links between health status and socio-economic inequalities have not disappeared; according to Giddens, 'some scholars believe that the relative health inequality between the richest and poorest members of society is widening' (2001:145). Research available for the Irish situation is consistent with international findings. 'The findings that poorer people, on average live shorter lives and are subject to more ill-health at an earlier age than their richer counterparts leads to what Nolan (1989:2) describes as 'a double injustice – life is short where quality is poor' (Quin 1999:28).

Ethnicity

There is evidence of a link between ethnicity and health status. Certain diseases are seen to affect ethnic groups differently, for example:

1. 'Sickle cell anaemia affects mainly Afro-Caribbeans.
2. Rickets affects mostly Asians.
3. Admission rates for mental illness are also higher for Afro-Caribbeans (with a much greater likelihood of a schizophrenia diagnosis)' (Macionis and Plummer 2002:522).

Some of these inequalities or differences in health status are a result of discrimination and racism. The Travelling community (Ireland's largest ethnic group) has been identified as having a particularly poor health status. 'The main cause of Travellers' inferior health status is to be found in poor living conditions, social exclusion and racism' (Tovey and Share 2003:285). Health services in Ireland have failed to address the specific needs of Travellers and this may have shaped their 'perceptions of, and responses to, ill health and health services' (Fanning 2002, cited in Tovey and Share 2003:285).

An understanding of the sociology of health and continued research on the health inequalities that exist (as a result of social factors, such as gender and class) will hopefully reduce differentials between socio-economic groups. The end result may be a health service that benefits all members of its society.

12

Demography and Urbanisation

CHAPTER OBJECTIVES

After reading this chapter you should be able to:
- define demography
- discuss the historical perspectives in relation to population
- describe the population structure in Ireland in terms of:
  - birth and death rates
  - life expectancy
  - infant mortality
  - migration – emigration and immigration
  - demographic changes and their relationships to individuals and society
- define what is meant by urbanisation
- describe the human impact on the environment.

DEMOGRAPHY DEFINED

'Demography is the study of human populations, particularly their size, structure and development' (O'Donnell 2002:215).

Demographers, that is, those who study trends in population, are concerned with measuring the size of populations and explaining their rise or decline. According to Clarke *et al.*, demography, the study of population, consists of two primary aspects: structures and processes:

1. Structures examine how the population is made up, for example how many single-parent families or people over eighty live in an area.
2. Processes examine the rate of change of variables such as births, deaths and migration. (2000:117)

'Demography is customarily treated as a branch of sociology because the factors influencing the level of births and deaths in a given group or society, as well as migrations of population, are largely social and cultural' (Giddens 2001:603).

Population patterns are governed by three factors: births, deaths and migrations. In 1950 the population of the world was 2.5 billion; this increased to 3.7 billion in 1970 and to 5.2 billion in 1990. In 1950, the population of Europe was 15.6 per cent of the world's total; this had decreased to 9.5 per cent in 1990 (Courtney 1995:39). In 1950 the annual growth in world population was twenty-eight million per year. This increased to seventy-two million by 1970. Statistics provided by the United Nations show that there were 5.3 billion in the world in 1991 and estimate that by the year 2050, this figure will have increased to ten billion people (Marsh 2000:517). According to Marsh, the biggest increase in population is expected to take place in Africa and Asia, areas of the developing world. 'The developed world commands the majority of the world's income, but its population at 1.2 billion is only twenty-nine per cent of that of the developing world' (2000:517).

HISTORICAL PERSPECTIVES: THEORIES OF POPULATION GROWTH

A number of theories have tried to explain the potential impacts of population growth. Two of these are the Malthusian Theory and Demographic Transition Theory.

1. **Malthusian Theory**: Thomas Malthus (1766–1834), an English clergyman, was the first to carry out a major systematic study of population. In his *Essay on Population* (1798), he claimed a 'law of population' – 'that the human species, when unchecked, goes on doubling itself every 25 years' (O'Connell 2002:215). His global argument was that population increases in a geometrical progression (1, 2, 4, 8, 16 . . .) while food supply or subsistence increases in an arithmetical progression (1, 2, 3, 4, 5) when conditions are favourable. Malthus believed that positive and preventive checks would slow the tide of population increase. Positive checks such as famine, disease and war slow down population increase due to increasing mortality. Preventive checks bringing about decreasing fertility are achieved by late marriage, sexual abstinence and family planning (Courtney 1995:40). Some used this theory to argue against improving the conditions of the poor, as doing so would only mean that more people will survive and this would speed up the collapse of the population (O'Donnell 2002:215).

2. **Demographic Transition Theory**: This theory directly opposes the ideas of Malthus. 'Whereas for Malthus increasing prosperity would automatically bring about population increase, the thesis of demographic transition emphasises that economic development generated by industrialism actually leads to a new equilibrium of population stability' (Giddens 2001:603). This

theory links demographic changes to a society's level of technological development and it attempts to answer questions such as why population increase is higher in poorer countries than in richer countries. It answers these questions 'by analysing birth and death rates at four stages of a society's technological development' (Macionis and Plummer 2002:603). These stages represent societies at different levels of industrialisation and technological development, for example:

Stage 1: Societies at this stage have not yet experienced industrialisation. These societies have high birth rates and high death rates. Birth rates are high because of the absence of effective family planning and because of the economic value of children. Low living standards, lack of medical technology, etc., are among the factors that contribute to a high death rate. Population increase at this stage is modest as deaths almost offset births.

Stage 2: This stage sees populations increase. It is characteristic of societies at the start of industrialisation. The advent of technology 'expands food supplies and science combats disease'. Rapid population growth occurs because death rates fall but birth rates remain high. 'Most of the world's least economically developed societies today are still in this high-growth stage' (*Ibid.*:603).

Stage 3: Societies at this stage are mature industrial economies. Birth rates drop as most children at this stage survive to adulthood and the cost of raising children increases. More and more women are working outside the home and there is widespread availability of contraception making family planning more effective. As birth rates follow death rates downward, population growth slows further.

Stage 4: This stage corresponds to a post-industrial economy. Both rates continue to fall and population growth is very slow.

This theory has been criticised on the grounds that 'current economic arrangements only ensure continued poverty in much of the world. Unless there is a significant redistribution of global resources . . . our planet will become increasingly divided into industrialised "haves", enjoying low population growth and non-industrialised "have nots", struggling in vain to feed soaring populations' (Macionis and Plummer 2002:603).

Malthus's prediction regarding the collapse of the population has not taken place. He underestimated the advances in industry, technology and communications that have occurred. 'Since 1950, the growth in world trade, the impact of the so-called "green revolution" in agriculture and the use of technology has prevented the type of global catastrophe predicted by Malthus from occurring' (Marsh 2000:518).

THE POPULATION STRUCTURE IN IRELAND

Demography, from the Greek words meaning 'description of people', provides statistical information on human populations. The components of population consist of birth and death and the natural movements of people – migrations. According to Quin, 'Ireland's demographic profile is changing in the same way as in other countries in the EU' (1999:29). Information on the demographics of a society is very important if we are to try and understand that society. 'The nature of human society cannot be fully understood without a clear comprehension of the integral role by population processes in the dynamics of social life' (Courtney 1995:39). The Central Statistics Office in Ireland collects, compiles and analyses population statistics. The census of population gathers demographic, social, economic and administrative data at a given time relating to all persons and households in a country (Ibid.:43). The following information provides an overview of the population structure in Ireland and the changes in the demographic patterns that have taken place here.

Birth rates

'Birth rate refers to the number of live births per 1000 of the population in a given year while death or mortality rate is the number of deaths per 1000 of the population in a given year' (O'Donnell 2002:223). According to figures from the Central Statistics Office (CSO), the population of Ireland was 4.13 million in April 2005. 'This figure is the highest on record since the census of 1861, which gave Ireland a population of 4.4 million' (CSO, cited in Humphreys 2005). In the year from April 2004 to April 2005 the population grew by 87,000. The natural increase in the population for that same year was 33,500, compared to 16,600 for the year 2003–4. According to the CSO, a factor in the population growth was 'a doubling in the excess of births over deaths in the past ten years' (cited in Humphreys 2005). These statistics provide evidence that Ireland has the fastest growing population in Europe.

In the 1920s Ireland's fertility rates were unusually high when compared to other European countries. 'Even as late as 1987, Ireland's fertility rate was the highest of any developed country with the exception of the former Soviet Union' (Coleman 1992, cited in Tovey and Share 2003:134). According to Tovey and Share:

- Ireland had the lowest proportion of first births and the highest proportion of births that were the fourth or subsequent child of the same mother.

- Ireland was the most youthful country in the industrialised world in the 1980s, with nearly one-third of its population under fifteen (2003:141). Between 1980 and 1996, Ireland's birth rate fell by about one-third. (Fitzgerald 1999:270)

Table 12:1 Average Annual Births, Deaths and Natural Increase for Each Intercensal Period 1926–2002

Period	Total births	Total deaths	Natural increase (000s)
1926–36	58	42	16
1936–46	60	43	17
1946–51	66	40	26
1951–56	63	36	27
1956–61	61	34	26
1961–66	63	33	20
1966–71	63	33	30
1971–79	69	33	35
1979–81	73	33	40
1981–86	67	33	34
1986–91	56	32	24
1991–96	50	31	18
1996–2002	54	31	23

(Adapted from CSO 2002:12)

There have been changes in the behaviour of Irish people in relation to birth, marriage and family formation. The following trends in fertility have emerged: 'smaller families, later motherhood, more voluntary childlessness, more single-parent families, more "only children" and more children born outside legal marriage' (Tovey and Share 2003:149).

Life expectancy

'The expectation of life is the average number of years a person can expect to live at a given age' (O'Donnell 2002:221). In Ireland the average life expectancy for men is 70.1 years and for women 75.6 years (Tovey and Share 2003:142).

Table 12:2 Population by Sex and Age Group 2002

Age Group	Males (000s)	Females (000s)
0–4 years	142.0	135.6
5–14	282.0	267.8
15–24	325.7	315.8
25–34	308.5	308.9
35–44	279.8	283.1
45–54	241.6	174.2
65–74	117.0	128.6
75–84	59.7	89.0
85 years and over	12.5	29.2
Total	1,946.2	1,971.0

(Adapted from CSO 2002:16)

The effects of lower female mortality are clear for age groups over sixty-five. For every 100 females aged over eighty-five years in 2002 there were less than forty-three males.

Infant mortality

'Refers to the number of deaths among infants under 1 year of age for each thousand live births in a given year' (Macionis and Plummer 2002:594). This is regarded as a good guide to the state of health and health services in a country.

Migration – emigration and immigration

Migration refers to the movement of people into and out of a particular territory. The eighteenth and early nineteenth centuries saw a huge growth in the population in Ireland but did not have an economic system to sustain it. In 1841 the population of Ireland was a little more than half that in England and Wales which had a population of 15.9 million. 'After the famines of the 1840s, Malthus's "idea" was achieved when the Irish population overall declined dramatically and continuously until 1926, from 8,177,744 to 4,228,553, by 48 per cent' (Courtney 1995:48). According to research by Geary (1951), Drudy (1995) and Ryan (1990), cited in Tovey and Share 2003:134–5):

- In the first half of the 1900s Ireland's population was the only one in the world which declined, with its excess of emigration over natural increase.
- More women emigrated than men.
- Between 1600 and 1922, seven million people left Ireland for North America. Four million left in the years from 1846 to 1925 (MacLaughlin 1994, cited in Tovey and Share 2003:145).
- Between 1890 and 1990, it is estimated that over two million Irish people emigrated to Britain.

Courtney estimates that up to a quarter of all Irish-born people live outside the country (1997, cited in Tovey and Share 2003:136–7).

'In recent years, Ireland has experienced a phenomenon that has been largely absent for most of its recent history: substantial immigration' (Tovey and Share 2003:155). With immigration rising to record levels, Ireland faces a dramatic change in its population composition as the number of foreign nationals living in the state approaches 400,000, accounting for eight to nine per cent of the population of 4.13 million (Humphreys 2005). A study by the CSO of population and migration estimates covering the period April 2004 to April 2005 showed that:

- one-third of immigrants to Ireland in that year came from the new accession states
- seventeen per cent of immigrants were from Poland (11,900)
- ten per cent of immigrants were from the UK (6,900)
- nine per cent of immigrants were from Lithuania (6,300)
- twelve per cent of immigrants were from other accession states (8,200)
- ten per cent of immigrants were from the rest of the EU 15 (7,100)
- two per cent of immigrants were from the USA (1,600)
- thirteen per cent of immigrants were from the rest of the world (9,000).

Historically, population patterns in Ireland have been affected by factors including emigration, low levels of urbanisation, low incomes, the dominance of rural livelihoods and private property relations and the influence of the Roman Catholic Church (Tovey and Share 2003:143). Modernisation of Irish society has resulted in population patterns that resemble the majority of western countries. According to Tovey and Share, 'now the patterns may be affected by trends such as higher educational levels, increasing costs of raising children for longer periods of time and the widespread entry of married women into the workforce' (2003:143).

Demographic changes and their relationships to individuals and society

'The impact of changing demography is of significance for the provision and development of different areas of Irish social policy in the coming decades' (Quin 1999:4). Changes in demography can put pressure on existing services within society. Population structures can affect health and social care priorities, education, welfare and housing. Estimates of current and future population structures form the basis of planning in these areas. Statistical information from census returns, surveys and the registration of births, deaths and marriages allows the demographic scientist to identify trends and make projections (Clarke *et al*. 2000:17). For example:

* According to Fitzgerald, 'a drop in the birth rate has brought a demographic dividend in the school system' (1999:270). A decline in the numbers of primary and secondary school students 'may provide opportunities to improve teacher/pupil ratios and to develop second-chance education to a much greater extent than is available presently' (Quin 1999:4).
* In April 2005 there were 111,300 people aged eighty years and over – a seventeen per cent increase over April 2000 (Humphreys 2005). An increase in the numbers of this age group is very likely to place increasing demands on health and on personal social services.
* Changes in the demographic pattern could cause difficulties in the housing area. 'An expanded generation in the household-forming age groups adds to pressure on house prices, which in turn increases the demand for social housing from those priced out of the private housing market' (Bacon 1998, cited in Fitzgerald 1999:270).

URBANISATION DEFINED

'Urbanisation – the process of living in and depending upon towns' (O'Donnell 2002:230).

Population increase and industrialisation have been linked to a growth of urban areas of unprecedented size. In 1975, thirty-nine per cent of the world's population lived in urban localities; this figure is predicted to be sixty-three per cent by 2025 (Giddens 2001:573). He believes that urban populations are growing much faster than the world's overall population. Industrialisation fuelled the growth of cities as people left the countryside and moved to cities in search of work. Urbanisation changed the physical environment and transformed many patterns of social life. According to Ferdinand Tonnies (1855–1936), urbanisation changed the basis and nature of social contacts. He noted a 'shift from Gemeinschaft or community characterised by close-knit, personal and stable relationships between friends and neighbours to . . . Gesellschaft or association based on transitory, instrumental relationships . . .' (cited in Bilton *et al.* 2002:38). Different types of cities emerged in the twentieth century. These included:

- megacities – cities with a population over eight million
- megalopolises – urban areas containing a number of cities and their surrounding areas.

O'Donnell (2002:241) lists the following as the advantages and disadvantages of urbanisation:

Advantages of urbanisation

1. greater access to educational and professional opportunities for more people
2. greater choice – more shops, pubs, clubs, etc.
3. reduced physical isolation
4. easier communications
5. greater cultural diversity.

Disadvantages of urbanisation

1. social isolation due to lack of close-knit, personal relationships
2. higher levels of crime and violence due to reduced common identity, less certainty of detection
3. more pollution, road congestion
4. less homogenous – differences among people create potential for conflict. (2002:241)

HUMAN IMPACT ON THE ENVIRONMENT

Human activity has had a harmful impact on the natural world. Two areas of major concern are:

1. pollution and waste products that are released into the environment, and
2. depletion of renewable resources. (Giddens 2001:573)

According to Giddens:

- Since 1960 consumption of fresh water has doubled.
- The burning of fossil fuels has almost quintupled in the past fifty years.
- In the last twenty-five years, the consumption of wood is up by forty per

cent. Organisations such as Greenpeace aim to raise awareness about environmental issues. People are being educated to conserve the earth's resources, to recycle and to keep pollution to a minimum.

- 'Population is one of today's most pressing concerns. The relationship between the number of people living on the planet and the resources to support their continued existence and welfare is a complex and dynamic one' (Tovey and Share 2003:134).

In conclusion, knowledge of a society's population structure and the changes that have occurred within it are necessary to identify social needs and to ensure services are developed to meet these needs. Updated demographic information and data 'constitute the basis for strategic economic and social planning and development throughout the public, voluntary and private sectors' (Courtney 1995:84).

Bibliography

1. Abbott, D. (1998) *Culture and Identity*, Hodder and Stoughton, England.
2. An Garda Síochána (2003) *Crime Statistics* [Internet]. Available from: http://www.usi.edu/libarts/socio/chapter/socialization/socialisation.ht ml> [accessed 12 October 2005]
3. Babbie, E. (1988) *The Sociological Spirit*, Wadsworth Publishing Company, California.
4. Bilton, T., Bonnett, K. and Jones, P. (2002) *Introductory Sociology*, 4th ed., Palgrave Macmillan, Great Britain.
5. Census (2002) available from: <http://www.cso.ie/statistics/population.htm> [accessed October 2005]
6. Central Statistics Office (2004) *Women and Men in Ireland* [Internet] Central Statistics Office. Available from: <http://www.cso.ie/releasepublications/documents/otherreleases/2004/ womenandmeninireland2004.pdf> [accessed September 2005]
7. Centre for Gypsy Research (1993) *The Education of Gypsy and Traveller Children*, University of Hertfordshire Press, England.
8. Clancy, P. (1999) 'Education Policy' in: Quin, S., Kennedy, P., O'Donnell, A. and Kiely, G. ed. *Contemporary Irish Social Policy*, University College Dublin Press, Dublin, pp. 72–107.
9. Clarke, L., Sachs, B. and Ford-Sumner, S. (2000) *Health and Social Care*, 3rd ed., Stanley Thornes, UK.
10. Cole, T., (1999) *Wealth, Poverty and Welfare*, Hodder and Stoughton, England.
11. Cormack, D., (2000) *The Research Process in Nursing*, 4th ed., Blackwell Science Ltd, Oxford.
12. Cotter, A. (1999) 'The Criminal Justice System in Ireland' in: Quin S., Kennedy, P., O'Donnell, A. and Kiely, G. ed. *Contemporary Irish Social Policy*, University College Dublin Press, Dublin, pp. 286–305.
13. Courtney, D. (1995) 'Demographic Structure and Change in the Republic of Ireland and Northern Ireland' in: Clancy, P., Drudy, S., Lynch, K. and O'Dowd, L. ed. *Irish Society: Sociological Perspectives*, Institute of Public Administration, Dublin, pp. 39–89.
14. Crowley, N. (1999) 'Travellers and social Policy' in: Quin, S., Kennedy, P., O'Donnell, A. and Kiely, G. ed. *Contemporary Irish Social Policy*,

University College Dublin Press, Dublin, pp. 243–62.

15. Donohoe, J. and Gaynor, F. (1999) *Education and Care in the Early Years*, Gill & Macmillan, Dublin.

16. Donohoe, J. and Gaynor, F. (2003) *Education and Care in the Early Years*, 2nd ed., Gill & Macmillan, Dublin.

17. Drudy, S., (1995) 'Class Society, Inequality and the Declassed' in: Clancy, P., Drudy, S., Lynch, K. and O'Dowd, L. ed. *Irish Society: Sociological Perspectives*, Institute of Public Administration, Dublin, pp. 295–323.

18. DTEDG (1992) *Irish Travellers: New Analysis and New Initiatives*, Pavee Point, Dublin.

19. Fahey, T. (1995) 'Family and Household in Ireland' in: Clancy, P., Drudy, S., Lynch, K. and O'Dowd, L. ed. *Irish Society: Sociological Perspectives*, Institute of Public Administration, Dublin, pp. 205–34.

20. Fitzgerald, E. (1999) 'Financing Social Services' in: Kiely, G., O'Donnell, A., Kennedy, P., and Quin, S. ed. *Irish Social Policy in Context*, University College Dublin Press, Dublin, pp. 269–92.

21. Giddens, A., (2001) *Sociology*, 4th ed., Polity Press, UK.

22. Hall, D. and Hall, I. (1996) *Practical Social Research*, Macmillan Press, London.

23. Haralambos, M. and Holborn, M. (2000) *Sociology: Themes and Perspectives*, HarperCollins, London.

24. Harvey, L., MacDonald, M. and Hill, J. (2000) *Theories and Methods*, Hodder and Stoughton, England.

25. Holdaway, S. (1988) *Crime and Deviance*, Macmillan Education, London.

26. Humphreys, J. (2005) 'Irish Population Growth Europe's Highest' says report, *The Irish Times*, 15 September, pp. 1, 3.

27. Institute of Public Administration (1992) *Sociology*, IPA, Dublin.

28. Kane, E. (1983) *Doing Your Own Research*, Turoe Press, Dublin.

29. Kennedy, F. (1997) 'The Course of the Irish Welfare State' in: Ó Muircheartaigh, F. ed. *Ireland in the Coming Times*, Institute of Public Administration, Dublin, pp. 129–55.

30. Lee, D. and Newby, H. (1986) *The Problem of Sociology*, Hutchinson Education, London.

31. LMU Learning Centre, 'Quote, Unquote' in: *The Harvard Style of Referencing Published Material*, Leeds Metropolitan University.

32. Lynch, K. and McLaughlin, E. (1995) 'Caring Labour and Love Labour' in: Clancy, P., Drudy, S., Lynch, K. and O'Dowd, L. ed. *Irish Society:*

Sociological Perspectives, Institute of Public Administration, Dublin, pp. 250–92.

33. Lynch, K. and Morgan, V. (1995) 'Gender and Education: North and South' in: Clancy, P., Drudy, S., Lynch, K. and O'Dowd, L. ed. *Irish Society: Sociological Perspectives*, Institute of Public Administration, Dublin, pp. 529–62.

34. Macionis, J. and Plummer, K. (1997) *Sociology, a Global Introduction*, Prentice Hall, Europe.

35. Macionis, J. and Plummer, K. (2002) *Sociology, a Global Introduction*, 2nd ed., Prentice Hall, Europe.

36. MacGreil, M. (1996) *Prejudice in Ireland Revisited*, St Patrick's College, Maynooth.

37. MacLaughlin, J. (1995) *Travellers and Ireland: Whose Country, Whose History?*, Cork University Press, Cork.

38. Mann, M. (1983) *Macmillan Student Encyclopaedia of Sociology*, The Macmillan Press, London.

39. Marsh, I. (2000) *Sociology: Making Sense of Society*, 2nd ed., Prentice Hall, England.

40. Marsh, I. (2002) *Theory and Practice in Sociology*, Pearson Education, England.

41. McCullagh, C. (1999) 'Crime and Punishment' in: *Studies*, Summer, pp. 126–31.

42. Modood, T. and Bethoud, R. (1997) *Ethnic Minorities in Britain: Diversity and Disadvantage*, Policy Studies Institute, London.

43. National Consultative Committee on Racism and Interculturalism (2005) *Traveller and Roma Community* [Internet]. Available from: <http://www.nccri.com/cdsu-travellers.html> [accessed 6 September 2005]

44. Conference on Planning Health and Social Care Services for the Elderly: Implications of the Projected Increase in our Elderly Population (1991–2011) 1995, National Council for the Elderly (1996) *Comments and Recommendations*, National Council for the Elderly, Dublin.

45. Ní Shuinear, S. (1996) 'Irish Travellers, Ethnicity and the Origins Question' in: McCann, M., Ó Síocháin, S. and Ruane, J. ed. *Irish Travellers: Culture and Ethnicity*, Queen's University, Belfast.

46. Noonan, P. (1996) 'Policy-making and Travellers in Northern Ireland' in: McCann, M., Ó Síocháin, S. and Ruane, J. ed. *Irish Travellers: Culture and Ethnicity*, Queen's University, Belfast.

47. O'Donnell, G. (2002) *Mastering Sociology*, 4th ed., Palgrave, New York.
48. O'Donnell, M. (1992) *A New Introduction to Sociology*, Nelson and Sons Ltd, Surrey.
49. O'Loughlin, A. (1999) 'Social Policy and Older People in Ireland' in: Quin S., Kennedy, P., O'Donnell, A. and Kiely, G. ed. *Contemporary Irish Social Policy*, University College Dublin Press, Dublin, pp. 221–42.
50. O'Mahony, P. (2000) 'Crime in the Republic of Ireland: A Suitable Case for Social Analysis', *Irish Journal of Sociology*, Volume 10, pp. 3–26.
51. Osborne, R. and van Loon, B. (1999) *Introducing Sociology*, Icon Books, Cambridge.
52. Parish of the Travelling People (2000) *Travellers: Citizens of Ireland*, Parish of the Travelling People, Dublin.
53. Pryke, S. (2002) 'The Nature of Social Theory' in: Marsh, I., ed. *Theory and Practice in Sociology*, Pearson Education, England, pp. 73–91.
54. Quin, S. (1999) 'Improving Health Care: Policy in Ireland' in: Quin S., Kennedy, P., O'Donnell, A. and Kiely, G. ed. *Contemporary Irish Social Policy*, University College Dublin Press, Dublin, pp. 27–48.
55. Rattansi, A. (1992) 'Changing the Subject? Racism, Culture and Education' in: Donald, J., and Rattansi, A. ed. *Race, Culture and Difference*, Sage Publications, London, pp. 11–48.
56. Richardson, V. (1999) 'Children and Social Policy' in: Quin, S., Kennedy, P., O'Donnell, A. and Kiely, G. ed. *Contemporary Irish Social Policy*, University College Dublin Press, Dublin, pp. 170–99.
57. Ritzer, G. (1992) *Sociological Theory*, 3rd ed., McGraw-Hill, US.
58. Robson, C. (2002) *Real World Research*, 2nd ed., Blackwell Publishers, UK.
59. Sclater, S. D. (2000) *Families*, Hodder and Stoughton, England.
60. Selfe, P. and Starbuck, M. (1998) *Religion*, Hodder and Stoughton, England.
61. Silke, D. (1999) 'Housing Policy' in: Quin, S., Kennedy, P., O'Donnell, A. and Kiely, G. ed. *Contemporary Irish Social Policy*, University College Dublin Press, Dublin, pp. 49–71.
62. 'Socialization: from Infancy to Old Age' [Internet]. Available from: http://www.usi.edu/libarts/socio/chapter/socialiazation/socialisation.html> [accessed 12 October 2005]
63. Task Force on the Travelling Community (1995) *Report of the Task Force on the Travelling Community*, Stationery Office, Dublin.
64. Thompson, I. (1986) *Sociology in Focus: Religion*, Longman Group, UK.
65. Tovey, H. and Share, P. (2000) *A Sociology of Ireland*, Gill and Macmillan, Dublin.

66. Tovey, H. and Share, P. (2003) *A Sociology of Ireland*, 2nd ed., Gill and Macmillan, Dublin.

67. Webb, R. and Tossell, D. (1999) *Social Issues for Carers: towards Positive Practice*, 2nd ed., Arnold Publishers, Great Britain.

68. Wood, K. and O'Shea, P. (1997) *Divorce in Ireland*, O'Brien Press Ltd, Dublin.

69. Wood, K. and O'Shea, P. (2003) *Divorce in Ireland: Marital Breakdown: Answers and Alternatives*, First Law Ltd, Dublin.

70. http://www.staffweb.itsligo.ie/staff/pshare/soci/family%20lecture.com [accessed October 2005]

71. http:www.LMU.ac.uk/155/15/docs/Harvard/Harvard.htm.